Copy 1

DATE DUE			

DRUG ABUSE:
The Impact
on Society

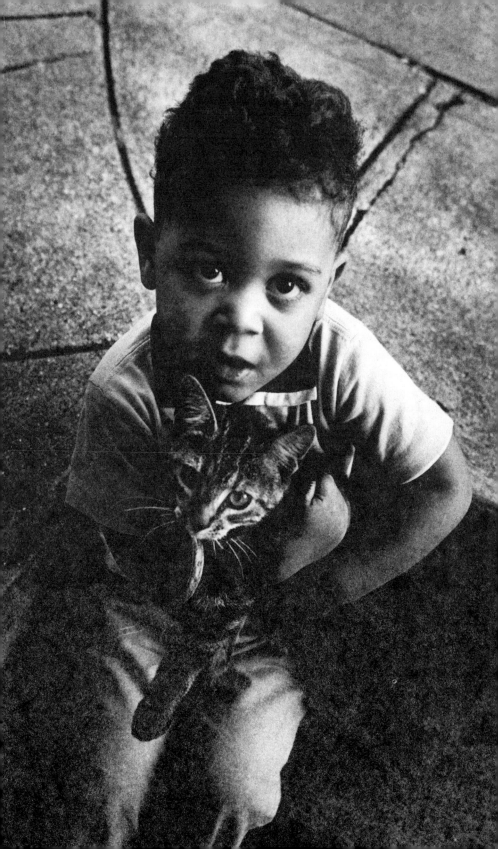

DRUG ABUSE
THE IMPACT ON SOCIETY

BY GILDA BERGER

FRANKLIN WATTS
NEW YORK/LONDON/
SYDNEY/TORONTO/1988

Frontis: "Little Julio" was born addicted;
he had to undergo withdrawal at birth.

Photographs courtesy of:
Photo Researchers: pp. 2 (Bob Combs), 30 (Fred
Mark Tosi), 81 (Guy Gilette); Sygma: pp. 10 and
121 (Tannenbaum); Monkmeyer: pp. 21 (Paul Conklin),
94 (Rick Kopstein); Gamma/Liaison: p. 46 (John
Chiasson); Comstock: p. 105; AP/Wide World: p. 111.

Library of Congress Cataloging-in-Publication Data
Berger, Gilda.
Drug abuse : the impact on society / by Gilda Berger.
p. cm.
Bibliography: p.
Includes index.
Summary: Discusses drug abuse and its impact on modern society in
such areas as crime, family life, and the work place.
ISBN 0-531-10579-2
1. Drug abuse—United States—Juvenile literature. 2. Drug abuse—
United States—Prevention—Juvenile literature. 3. Drug abuse and
crime—United States—Juvenile literature. 4. Narcotics, Control
of—United States—Juvenile literature. [1. Drug abuse.]
I. Title.
HV5825.B48 1988
362.2'93'0973—dc19 88-10620 CIP AC

CONTENTS

DRUG ABUSE: The Impact on Society

1
INTRODUCTION

Peter is seventeen years old and lives at home in southern California. He has been smoking and drinking beer since he was ten years old. When he was thirteen, he started smoking joints of marijuana. At fifteen he began doing drugs almost every day.

Peter became so disruptive in school that he was put into a special class. When he continued to cause trouble, the principal barred him from school. Because of his failing grades and the suspension, Peter decided to drop out of school altogether.

To support himself, Peter took a succession of jobs—pumping gas, helping on a delivery truck, and cleaning up in a fast-food restaurant. But none of these positions lasted very long. Either he showed up for work stoned, came late too many times, or just failed to appear.

Soon Peter turned to stealing. At first he just took small sums from people he knew—parents, friends, and relatives. But then he began robbing houses in the neighborhood. Twice he was picked up by the police, but each time they let him go.

As a result of his last arrest, though, Peter had to enroll in a local drug-rehabilitation program. Although he continued to live at home, he went to the clinic every day. The therapy included individual meetings

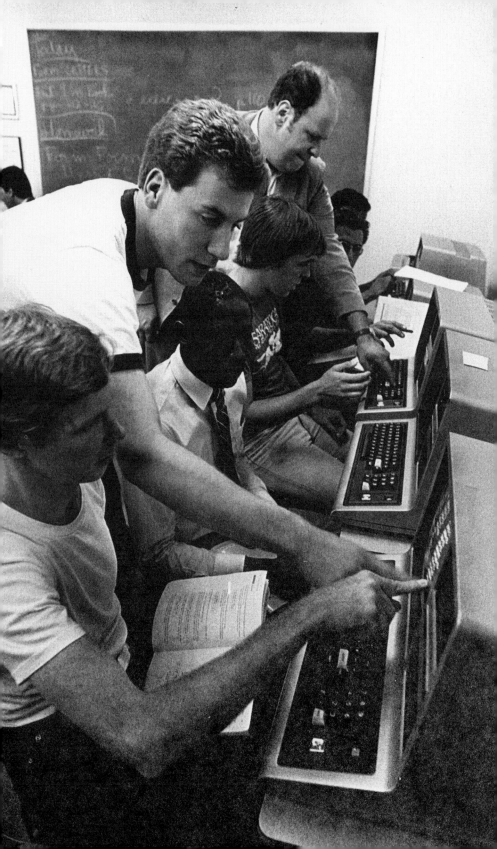

with drug counselors and group sessions with other drug addicts to work through common problems.

For weeks Peter attended the program every day and stayed off drugs. But then one evening he went out for a beer with some friends. They began passing around a joint. At first, Peter refused. But on second thought he decided, "One joint won't hurt me," and took a couple of puffs.

One thing led to another. In no time at all he was back on drugs. He began skipping appointments at the clinic. Then, he stopped going altogether.

The next time Peter was arrested, his dad refused to bail him out. This made his mother distraught and ill. She wanted him home. His parents argued and fought until Peter's father finally gave in. The present situation with his parents is tense and uneasy.

For people like Peter, his family, and all those with whom he has contact, life is a never-ending series of problems and crises. The jobs he gets, he loses. His petty crimes lead to arrests, trials, and possible prison terms. And his many hopeful starts in treatment programs usually end in dismal failure.

The fact is, there are millions of "Peters" in America. All of them—men and women, young and old, rich and poor, white, black, or Hispanic, in big cities or small towns—are alike in one way. They hurt themselves and others through the abuse of drugs.

Most drug abusers try to keep their drug habits to themselves. "It's no one's business," they say. "What difference is it to you if I do drugs?"

Learning to operate a computer serves as both an activity and an educational opportunity for recovering drug abusers at a rehabilitation center in New York.

The answer is that drug abuse makes a very *big* difference to each and every one of us. Drug abuse tears apart the family. Disruptive behavior in school makes it impossible for teachers to teach and students to learn. Getting and losing jobs makes it hard for employers to run their businesses. Stealing causes pain and loss to the victims. Arrests and jailings strain the criminal justice system and cost taxpayers huge sums of money. The money spent on illegal drugs supports a large criminal class and robs the government of millions in lost tax revenues.

Drug abuse is a widespread problem. The individual drug users are the prime victims. But drugs also impinge on every aspect of our entire society.

OVERVIEW OF THE PROBLEM

Drugs are all around us. Some, like alcohol and tobacco, are legal and are generally accepted, even though they have highly dangerous effects. Other substances, like marijuana, heroin, cocaine, barbiturates, LSD, and PCP are both dangerous *and* illegal. When taken alone, or with other substances, they may have severe effects on the user.

Although there is no question that alcohol remains the number-one drug of abuse in America, the emphasis in this book is on the abuse of illegal, also called illicit, drugs. According to a recent government survey, nearly 37 million Americans, about one out of every five people twelve years of age or older, have used one or more illegal drugs at some time. Americans now consume 60 percent of the world's illegal drugs.[1]

The numbers of young people involved in illicit drug use is especially staggering and poses the most acute problem. According to a 1986 survey by the government's National Institute on Drug Abuse (NIDA), by their mid-twenties, "some 75 to 80 percent of today's young adults have tried an illicit drug." More than half have tried an illicit drug other than marijuana. A country-wide survey of high school seniors stated that "this nation's high school students to young adults still show a level of involvement with illicit drugs which is greater than can be found in any other industrialized nation in the world."[2]

The full extent of the problem appears mixed. Overall, statistics show a leveling off or decline in most drug use, except for cocaine. But at the same time, drug abuse among the poor and ethnic minorities seems to be rising. Dr. David Musto, professor of psychiatry and history of medicine at Yale University, said, "In the inner city, the factors that counterbalance drug use—family, employment, status within the community—often are not there. It is harder for people with nothing to say no to drugs. Studies show that better-educated people are turning away from drugs while the poor and less-educated have continued or increased their drug use."[3]

Evidence that drug abuse is becoming more and more of a lower-class problem comes from both coasts of the United States. The New York State Division of Substance Abuse Services as well as the Los Angeles Office of Drug Abuse report that most of the crack users they treat are poor members of minority groups. James Hall, director of Up Front Drug Information, Inc. in Miami shares this finding: "Crack seems to have become entrenched in the inner-city areas."[4]

As drug addiction becomes more a problem of the poor than the middle class, some experts fear that funds to fight the problem will dry up. As Dr. Mitchell S. Rosenthal, president of Phoenix House, the drug treatment centers in New York and Los Angeles, said, "In the heroin crisis of the late 1960s, and again with crack in recent years, it was the threat to the middle- and upper-middle-class kids that put pressure on legislators and Congress. There is a danger that if they [legislators and Congress] feel less of a threat, the resources won't stay with the problem."[5]

Added to the bad effects of drugs on the young and the poor is the high incidence of AIDS among intravenous drug users. By sharing the needles they use to inject heroin into their veins, an alarming number of addicts are exposing themselves to the deadly virus that causes Acquired Immune Deficiency Syndrome (AIDS). While just a small percentage of drug abusers will die from drug overdose, most victims of AIDS will die of the disease. Dr. Beny J. Primm of the Addiction Research and Treatment Corporation in New York City reports that more than half the heroin addicts in drug treatment in New York already have the AIDS virus!

A CLOSER LOOK

Some experts have compared the use of illegal drugs in today's world to the spread of a plague during the Middle Ages:

- 56 million Americans have used marijuana.
- Up to 20 million have tried cocaine or crack one or more times.
- At least one million men and women abuse tranquilizers, barbiturates, or other sedative drugs every day.
- One-half million are addicted to heroin.
- Over one million are completely dependent on one or more illegal, or illicit, substances.[6]

Research shows that these drugs are now cheaper, purer, and far more plentiful than ever before. Despite a trend among young people to reduce their use of drugs, the rise of a new drug or something unpredictable could completely change the situation. And no matter what happens, experts expect widespread drug use to remain a problem for years to come.

The adverse effects of illegal drugs on the body include disease, disability, and even death. Drugs can also damage the user mentally and emotionally. They can lead to dependency, or addiction—a habitual or compulsive need to have the drug.

Drug abuse is also linked to much crime and violence in our towns and cities. A 1986 survey in New York City and Washington, D.C. found that 56 percent of criminal suspects who were tested were using drugs at the time of arrest. A recent Justice Department report showed that heroin addicts committed at least 100,000 burglaries, robberies, and auto thefts every single day. That totals about 20 percent of *all* property crimes in the country. If we add the property crimes committed by other addicts, we can probably double that number, according to Joseph A. Califano, Jr., former secretary of the Department of Health, Education, and Welfare.[7]

Employers are well aware that between 5 and 13 percent of the work force uses drugs. And they know that this drug abuse costs their companies an estimated $100 billion in lost productivity, absenteeism, higher accident rates, and increased health-care costs.[8]

Rampant drug use in the United States makes smuggling, trafficking, and dealing very lucrative. The sheer dollar volume of narcotics traffic is estimated at anywhere from $27 to $110 billion a year.[9] Drug distribution removes billions of dollars every year from the legal economy of the United States and passes it on to the drug underworld. Every year more than 150 tons (132,969 kg) of cocaine, 65 tons (58,967 kg) of marijuana, and 12 tons (10,886 kg) of heroin are spread across the land by an army of drug dealers, from the mighty drug lords to the street-corner pushers.[10] In Florida, trafficking has grown so phenomenally in recent years that it has become the biggest source of income in the state.[11]

President Ronald Reagan warned that "drugs are menacing our society." He called for a "national crusade" against drug abuse, and on October 27, 1986, signed into law a $1.7 billion antidrug bill. The legislation authorized stricter enforcement of existing drug laws, approved tougher penalties for various drug crimes, and increased the power of police officers to search and arrest individuals for drug use. In addition, the President instructed Cabinet officers and department heads to begin mandatory drug testing of those of the 2.8 million federal civilian employees who worked in sensitive jobs.

This so-called crusade against drugs still has a long way to go. Joseph P. Riley, mayor of Charleston, South Carolina, said, "Cities of all sizes, in all regions, are engaged in a war against inner-city pushers and international traffickers, and we are losing."[12] The flow of drugs and the rate of drug-related crime show little change. From 1985 to 1986, the smuggling of cocaine doubled in volume (75 to 150 tons) [68,039 to 136,077 kg], heroin traffic went up 20 percent (10 to 12 tons) [9,072 to 10,886 kg], and marijuana showed a 10 percent increase (59 to 65 tons) [53,524 to 58,967 kg]—all despite increased efforts at control.[13]

It has been said that a society abundant in illegal drugs is a society in the process of dismantling itself. You may not be able to stop the supply of drugs. But you can prevent it from involving you and the people you care about. One way is by learning about the great impact of drugs on American life.

2
THE SOCIAL HISTORY OF DRUGS

Scholars believe that societies experience drug epidemics in historical cycles. From 1885 to 1920, the United States had a problem with drug abuse as great as that of today. Around the turn of the century, doctors freely dispensed such dependence-producing drugs as cocaine, morphine, and heroin. The doctors were just as eager to show off their ability to stop pain as patients were to get instant relief. The same drugs were also readily available from a totally unregulated patent medicine industry. In addition, hucksters pushed quack medications of all kinds on an unsuspecting public.

In a series of articles called "The Great American Fraud," Samuel Hopkins Adams wrote in 1905:

> *Gullible America will spend this year $75 million in the purchase of patent medicines. In consideration of this sum it will swallow huge quantities of alcohol, an appalling amount of opiates and narcotics, a wide assortment of varied drugs ranging from powerful and dangerous heart depressants to insidious liver stimulants; and, far in excess of other ingredients, undiluted fraud. For fraud, exploited by the skillfulest of advertising bunco men, is the basis of the trade.*[1]

The Harrison Act, passed in 1914, made the use of certain drugs an illegal activity. The law required addicts and all who distributed cocaine and narcotics to register with the Treasury Department. It became a punishable violation to obtain these drugs in any way, even if prescribed by a doctor. Physicians became unwilling to treat addicts under any circumstances. An illegal drug marketplace emerged to meet the needs of people who were already on drugs.

Added to the effects of legislation, then, was the creation of a new class of users who were forced into the underworld. An article in the *New York Medical Journal* of 1914 reads:

> *Several individuals have come to the conclusion that selling "dope" is a very profitable business. These individuals have sent their agents among the gangs frequenting our city corners, instructing them to make friends with the members and induce them to take the drug. Janitors, bartenders, and cabmen have also been employed to help sell the habit. The plan has worked so well that there is scarcely a poolroom in New York that may not be called a meeting place for dope fiends. The drug has been made up in candy and sold to school children. The conspiring individuals, being familiar with the habit-forming action of the drugs, believe that the increased number of "fiends" will create a larger demand for the drug, and in this way build up profitable business.*[2]

By the early 1920s, drug use, especially heroin, was considered a national epidemic. Commentators blamed the problem on the greed of drug traffickers and the personality defects of the users. The call for more legislation led to passage of the Jones Miller Act (1922) that set fines of up to $5,000 and imprisonment of up to ten years for anyone involved in the trafficking of narcotics.

In the 1930s, a host of medical, police enforcement, and legislative efforts curbed the tide of narcotic addiction—for a while, at least. But it was during this time that marijuana began flooding the market. It was originally smoked by Mexican immigrants who came north looking for jobs. But within a few years marijuana was placed in the same illegal category as opium and cocaine.

By the beginning of the next decade, however, large-scale drug-taking had all but disappeared. The success was not due to the various laws and treatment facilities that had been opened. Rather, World War II had cut off supply routes of drugs from Asia and Europe. As an editorial in *Time* put it in 1942, "The war is probably the best thing that ever happened to U.S. drug addicts."[3]

The late 1940s witnessed the reappearance of opium-heroin trafficking networks and once again shipments of illegal narcotics began to reach America. Still, the prevailing image of drug use was one of dope fiends and addicts on dark city streets.

Although the 1950s were a period of prosperity, a number of social problems figured prominently. A mass migration to the suburbs helped lead to the deterioration of the inner cities. An overwhelming reliance on the automobile resulted in a breakdown in mass transportation. This led, in turn, to increased pollution and congestion. Racism persisted and American youth "faced an enforcement of conformity, a transparency of sexual morals, and a set of cultural prescriptions and proscriptions that stressed achievement, prejudice, waste, and compliance, and consensus, yet failed to explain or recognize the confusion and absurdity of it all."[4]

These developments led to one of the most revolutionary periods in recent history—the 1960s. About 1965, in what is termed the "drug revolution," drugs moved from the more marginal parts of society—the inner-city ghettos and underground "arty" cultures—to the very mainstream of community life, attracting adolescent middle-class and young-adult populations of both rural and urban America.

FROM 1965 ON

Students and young people embraced drugs to protest the "sterile conformity" of the past and to make a statement of personal freedom. Anger and defiance over the war in Vietnam also contributed to the rising use of drugs. Says National Cocaine Hotline's Dr. Arnold Washton, "Marijuana had a meaning beyond just getting high. It was the source of shared identity among people who had a common point of view, notably that their parents were stupid, that Government was immoral, and that the war in Vietnam was wrong."[5]

By the end of the 1960s, drug-taking had become a fixed part of American social life. "Turning on" to drugs in a vain search for relaxation and to share friendship and love became a commonplace activity.

Heroin remained the most feared drug throughout the 1960s. But strong stimulants, the amphetamines, also came to the forefront. When legislators tried to dry up amphetamine use, youthful users simply turned to other widely available drugs—quaaludes. Thus, one drug problem was replaced by another. And the heroin epidemic continued.

Young people experimenting with drugs in Washington, D.C., at a time of rising drug use

By the early 1970s, marijuana use had increased throughout all levels of society. Some policemen and plumbers, schoolteachers and carpenters, doctors and librarians—even some legislators—were smoking joints of marijuana.

There were an estimated 50 million users of marijuana in the United States by the end of the 1970s. As stated previously, by the onset of the 1980s, marijuana use actually began to decline—the figure dropped to 20 million users. Over the period from 1977 through 1986, the proportion of high school seniors in the United States smoking marijuana dropped from 35.4 percent to 23.4 percent.[6]

But now cocaine began to emerge as the new drug of choice. The percentage of daily cocaine users tripled from 1975 to 1986, from 1.9 to 6.2 percent. "Even by historical standards in this country, these rates are extremely high," concluded a survey by the University of Michigan Institute for Social Research as reported in the *New York Times*.[7]

Today, as America moves toward the end of the 1980s, substance abuse remains rampant. Many problems remain to be solved. Legislation has not had the intended effect of eliminating the use of dangerous drugs. As many users seem to have started using drugs because they are illegal as have avoided them for the same reason.

Legislation designed to eliminate drugs may well have created an increased supply. The laws passed over the years put the control of drug supplies into the hands of a very few major drug distributors. They were able to raise prices and increase their profits many times over. The huge amounts of money to be made attracted additional traffickers and dealers, vastly increasing the supply and hooking more people into heavy drug habits.

The disruption of American life due to drug abuse is enormous. Millions of drug users are forced to live as criminals in constant fear of arrest and prison; fortunes are made suddenly and illicitly; lives are ruined by drug dependence and drug overdoses; valuable resources, both human and material, are being wasted or destroyed; and an immense and powerful criminal empire has spread violence and corruption throughout the country.

There is widespread—and justified—alarm at what drugs are doing to the American nation, its people, and our society. But before discussing the reasons for concern, let's take a closer look at the particular illicit substances that are at the root of the drug-abuse crisis.

3

THE
ILLEGAL DRUGS

Each day millions of Americans swallow, smoke, or inject powerful mind- and mood-changing drugs into their bodies. Drug users call this "doing" drugs; experts call it "slow motion suicide."

People start taking illegal drugs for a few reasons: Drugs make them feel good. Drugs are accepted as part of our culture. And drugs are easily available. As a result we have become, to a large extent, a society hooked on drugs.

A Rand Study shows that children learn from television and imitate the behaviors that they see. What happens when young people see ads for legal drugs showing people getting relief from just about any pain or discomfort "in just seconds"? It creates the impression that drugs are the good, fast, sensible way to get relief from anything that bothers you. And that it is foolish not to feel good all the time—with the help of the various drugs.[1]

Many of today's kids—like a lot of grown-ups—think that it's all right to take drugs, legal or illegal, to get rid of bad feelings. They imagine that drugs will make them feel better. Further, they believe it will give them the feeling of belonging to a group, of being more readily accepted by others, of having more fun, and of being happier in general. Among the other reasons people give for saying yes to drugs is a desire to escape from pain, stress, frustration, or boredom, to rebel against authority, or just to satisfy their curiosity.

What exactly are these illegal drugs? What do they look like and how are they used?

NARCOTICS

Narcotics are substances that kill pain. Some narcotics are legal medical drugs. They include morphine, meperidine, perogorie (which contains opium), and cough syrups that contain codeine. They come in a variety of forms including capsules, tablets, syrups, solutions, and suppositories. Other narcotics, including opium, morphine, heroin, and methadone, are illegal drugs. Narcotics are either made from the poppy plant or are manufactured in factories from synthetic chemicals.

Opium was one of the first narcotics to be used. But smoking opium did more than stop pain. It also made users feel good and brought on sleep. In time, people began taking opium for the pleasant high it produced and forgot about its pain-killing purpose.

Heroin, which is also called "junk," "smack," or "horse," gives users the biggest "kick" of all the narcotics. Heroin makes worries and problems seem less important. It makes fear and tension fade away. Today, heroin accounts for 90 percent of the narcotic abuse in the United States.[2]

Heroin is usually a white or brownish powder with a sharp, bitter taste. Some users sniff the powder into the nose. But more often they dissolve the powder in water, which they then heat in a spoon held over a match flame and inject into a blood vessel in the arm.

Heroin sold on the street is almost always mixed with sugar, starch, or powdered milk. This makes the heroin weaker and provides even greater profits for those who sell this dangerous substance.

Regular use of heroin is habit-forming. It also builds up a tolerance for the drug in the user. That is, people using heroin must take larger and larger amounts of the drug to get the same result. Or, they feel they have to take another drug or alcohol with the heroin for a good high. And because heroin is very expensive and the desire for the drug can be very strong, some abusers feel forced to rob and steal to support their habit.

Heroin use has not increased significantly over the past decade. But experts are now worried about new trends in its use. One trend is to use heroin of even greater purity. "Black tar" and "China white" are two types of heroin that are up to 99 percent pure. They are believed to be largely responsible for the recent rise in deaths among addicts who are accustomed to a weaker drug. Also, some researchers fear that the growing popularity of smoking heroin, which makes needles unnecessary, may add to the number of addicts.

Another trend concerns the use of heroin in association with crack, a form of cocaine. Crack users, especially those who "binge" on the drug for several days, sometimes need a depressant to reduce and control the stimulating effects of cocaine. "People are looking for a chemical parachute to come off that racing high," says Dr. Mitchell S. Rosenthal, president of Phoenix House. "Heroin may become their final resting place."[3]

Since 1981, heroin addicts who inject the drug have had to face a new situation. Intravenous, or IV, heroin users often share the same hypodermic needles with other addicts. In this way they can pass on the AIDS virus from one individual to another.

AIDS is a serious, communicable illness that destroys the body's immune system. The immune system gives people their resistance and ability to fight infection. Without normal resistance, the person infected with the AIDS virus is liable to fall victim to a number of life-threatening diseases and infections.

The AIDS virus gets from one IV drug abuser to another through the needles they share. Even the smallest amount of infected blood left in a used needle can contain live AIDS viruses, which can then infect the next drug user.

COCAINE AND CRACK

Cocaine is a drug made from the leaves of the coca plant that grows in South America. Known on the street as "coke" or "snow," cocaine can give users a very powerful "flash" or "rush." That is, they quickly get a short burst of strength and good feeling from using the drug.

Cocaine appears in several different forms. It is usually a fine white powder that is sniffed or snorted into the nose. The drug can also be dissolved in water and injected directly into a muscle or vein. Or it can be smoked in a form known as crack.

Crack is a purified form of cocaine that is especially strong and addictive. Smoking crack produces a shorter and more intense high than any other way of using the drug. That is because smoking is the most direct and rapid way to get the drug to the brain. Since larger amounts are reaching the brain more quickly, smoking crack also increases the basic risks of using cocaine.

Injecting and smoking cocaine carry the greatest possibilities of harm. But any method can easily lead to a serious addiction—and possibly death.

AMPHETAMINES

The street names for amphetamines are "pep pills," "speed," "uppers," "dexies," or "bennies." In their pure form, they are yellowish crystals that are usually prepared in tablet or capsule form. Abusers either swallow or sniff the powdered crystals or make a solution for injections.

Amphetamines are stimulants. They give the user a high, a feeling of joy and elation, of strength and power. The user believes that there is nothing he or she cannot do. This high, though, is usually soon followed by a downside "crash" and depression.

Student athletes are often under a lot of pressure to succeed at sports. Some may turn to cocaine or amphetamines to get up for a game, relieve pain, celebrate a victory, or forget a defeat. Eventually, the dangers of these drugs become obvious.

People who use large amounts of amphetamines over a long time may begin seeing, hearing, and feeling things that do not exist (hallucinations), have irrational thoughts or beliefs (delusions), and feel that people are out to get them (paranoia). These sensations usually disappear when amphetamine use stops.

MARIJUANA

Marijuana, also known as "grass," "pot," or "weed," is the most widely used illegal drug. The figures actually show that marijuana use among high school students is going down. But in a 1986 survey, nearly one-fourth of the students still said that they had used the drug recently.[4]

Marijuana is made from the leaves and flowers of the Indian hemp plant called *Cannabis sativa*. When burned, it produces more than two thousand chemicals. Every puff brings these chemicals into the smoker's lungs and body and sends them around to every cell.

The main mind-altering (psychoactive) ingredient in marijuana, the one that gives users a high, is THC (delta-9-tetrahydrocannabinol). The percentage of THC in the drug has been increasing over the years. Ten years ago the average marijuana contained 0.2 percent THC. Today it is 5 percent. And, of course, the more THC, the stronger the high.

Most Americans smoke marijuana in the form of loosely rolled cigarettes, called "joints" or "reefers." Sometimes the marijuana is smoked in a pipe. Often, smokers pass a joint or pipe from person to person, each one taking a puff. Even one puff of marijuana sends a good deal of THC into the body.

It takes up to a week for the body to break down and excrete the THC. The exact time depends on the strength of the marijuana and the number of joints smoked. A person has to stop smoking for about a month to get rid of all the marijuana in the body.

Hashish, or "hash," is made by taking the resin from the leaves and flowers of the marijuana plant and pressing it into cakes or slabs. Hash contains five to ten times as much THC and is much stronger than the usual marijuana.

HALLUCINOGENS

Hallucinogens are mind-altering substances that are also called psychedelics. They change a person's perceptions, sensations, thinking, self-awareness, and emotions in special ways. PCP, LSD, and mescaline are the best known hallucinogens. They produce hallucinations, as well as delusions and distortions of time and space.

Most often called "angel dust," PCP (phencyclidine) was first developed as an anesthetic in the 1950s. It was, however, taken off the market for human use because of its dangerous side effects—delirium, extreme excitement, and visual disturbances.

PCP is sold on the street in a pure, white powdered form or as tablets or pills. The powder is sometimes

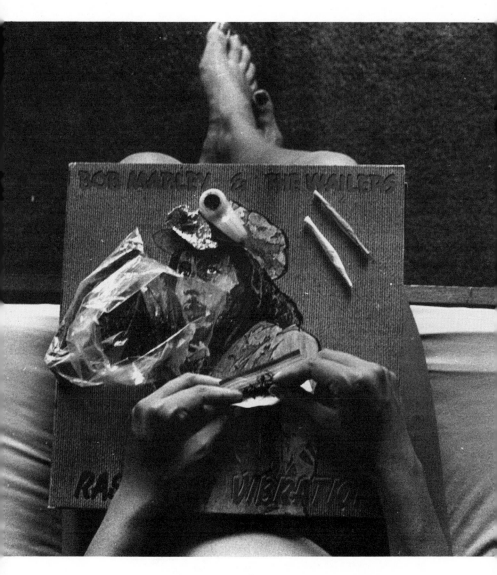

A woman uses an album cover as a surface to roll her homegrown marijuana. According to many, reggae music, such as that performed by the musician Bob Marley and his group, is associated with marijuana.

mixed with marijuana, parsley, or mint leaves, and tobacco. Other times small cigars, called "Shermans," are dipped in a PCP solution and smoked.

LSD (scientific name—lysergic acid diethylamide; street name—"acid") is either made synthetically or prepared from lysergic acid, which is found in ergot, a fungus that grows on rye and other grains. Discovered in 1938, it is one of the most potent mood-changing chemicals. Just one ounce of liquid can provide 300,000 average doses! The substance is odorless, colorless, and tasteless. Almost all street LSD contains impurities and adulterants—some dangerous.

LSD is sold in pill or tablet form, or as a liquid. The liquid may be dripped on a sugar cube, cracker, or cookie and then eaten. Often it is added to absorbent paper, such as blotter paper, and divided into small squares, which are then sold separately.

Mescaline is made from the peyote cactus. It may be smoked or swallowed in the form of capsules or tablets. Although mescaline is not as strong as LSD, its effects are similar.

SEDATIVES

Sedatives are drugs that depress, or slow down, the body's functions. They calm people who are nervous or agitated. Another name for sedatives is depressants or "downers."

In small doses sedatives quiet and relax the user; large doses put the user to sleep. Tranquilizers are one type of sedative. Among the best-known tranquilizers are Valium and Librium. People are usually given tranquilizers to handle stress and strain and cope with their fears and anxieties. Although the tranquilizers are legal drugs prescribed by physicians, they are often obtained illegally and abused.

It is estimated that one in every ten adults in the United States takes either Valium or Librium. Of these, about 68 percent are women. For some time it was believed that these were safe drugs, with little danger of overdose or dependency. Now, experts say that the tranquilizers do pose risks, with a likelihood of dependency after regular use for six weeks or so and up to ten days of withdrawal symptoms upon stopping.

Sleeping pills, or barbiturates, as their name indicates, calm people and put them to sleep. In very small amounts, barbiturates can quiet nervousness and anxiety. If more are taken, the drugs promote drowsiness. At very high doses these drugs may cause unconsciousness and death.

Barbiturates are often called "barbs." Their effects are, in many ways, similar to the effects of alcohol. Little doses produce calmness and a relaxed state. Somewhat larger doses can cause slurred speech, staggering gait, poor judgment, and slow, uncertain reflexes. These effects make it dangerous to drive a car or operate machinery. Large amounts can cause unconsciousness and death.

Quaalude (or "lude") is the trade name for methaqualone, another type of sedative. Originally prescribed by doctors to reduce anxiety during the day and help the patient sleep at night, it has now become a commonly abused drug. Quaaludes also produce effects like alcohol. They reduce inhibitions, making the users feel free to do things that they would not normally do. As effective painkillers, the "ludes" can also cause physical and psychological dependence. The dangers from abusing Quaalude include injury or death from accidents caused by faulty judgment and drowsiness, and convulsions, coma, and death from overdose.

These, then, are the most popular illegal drugs of the late 1980s. Let's see how they affect those who take them and what impact they make on our society.

4
HEALTH AND PERSONALITY EFFECTS

The ambulance made a fast, sharp turn at the brightly lit red-and-white sign, "Emergency Room." With siren still wailing and lights flashing, it screeched to a stop at the big glass doors. The driver rushed out as the paramedic, who had been riding in the back with the patient, flung open the doors. Together they slid out the stretcher with a ghostly figure on it. Almost running, they quickly rolled the stretcher through the glass doors that opened as they approached.

Within seconds a young doctor was at the patient's side. "What's the story?" he asked the paramedic as he reached for the unconscious man's pulse.

"We got this call from the cops," the paramedic answered. "This guy—Michael is his name—was tearing apart a supermarket. He was punching anyone who came near him, throwing cans through the window, and laughing and screaming all the time. Then, all of a sudden, he stopped dead in his tracks and collapsed. And that's the way we found him."

By now the doctor had taken Michael's pulse and temperature. "Pulse—200. Temperature—107 degrees. My God!" the doctor exclaimed.

The paramedic continued his account. "When we arrived, Michael's friend was with him. She said they had been doing crack since early this morning. Then they went to the store to get some beer and food. And that's when Michael suddenly went crazy."

For the next two hours the doctor worked on Michael, trying to revive him. But Michael never regained consciousness. The doctor transferred the victim to the intensive care unit for more tests and additional treatment.

Over the next days, the doctors struggled to keep Michael alive and to counter the killing effects of all the crack he had gotten into his system. But despite all their efforts, Michael died on his sixth day in the hospital.

Every day, in hospitals all over the country, people arrive at emergency rooms with various kinds of conditions brought on by drug abuse. Some are unconscious, like Michael. Others are suffering fits or convulsions. Some are having terrifying, realistic hallucinations. Still more cannot breathe or they feel their heart is beating so strongly that it will burst their chest. A few are in a stupor, unable to talk or move. Numbers show up complaining of severe pain.

Drug abusers almost never consider the health effects of the drugs they are taking. Their thoughts are just on the "magical" things that drugs can do. Take a drug when you're feeling down and you're up again. Take a drug when you're tense and nervous and suddenly you're calm and relaxed. Take a drug when you're bored or depressed and within minutes the world seems to be an exciting place.

But as you know, each drug poses a different health risk to the user. The 3,600 drug treatment centers and the hundreds of thousands of visits to hospital emergency rooms and doctors' offices for illnesses caused by drugs attest to the fact that drug abuse is damaging the health of the nation's citizens. It has put a terrible burden on the country's health care system, and is drawing vast numbers of doctors, health workers, and health dollars away from treating and curing illness unrelated to drug use.

HEALTH DISORDERS

Marijuana is by far the most popular of the illegal drugs. While its long-term effects are still under study, we now know marijuana is by no means harmless.

For one thing, the active chemicals in marijuana are fat soluble. That is, the drug is stored in the body's fat cells, and may stay there for as long as three weeks!

Researchers have also discovered that, besides remaining in the body for a long time, marijuana affects virtually every system and part of the body. It interferes with the electrical circuits within the brain, leading to difficulties with memory, learning, and perception. And some experts suspect that these changes may become permanent with long-time use.

Marijuana throws off the reproductive system and the amount of sex hormones the body produces. It is also linked to cancer, to the ability of the body to fight infection, to degeneration of the liver, to increased likelihood of respiratory diseases such as asthma and bronchitis, and to problems with the user's eyes and ears.

Psychological changes also can occur with heavy marijuana use. The users frequently show wild mood swings. They are happy and joyful one minute, angry and irritable the next. First they want to be with others, then they need to be by themselves. Fearful and anxious feelings soon follow sensations of relaxation and abandon. Occasionally, abusers of marijuana have bizarre hallucinations or become secretive and withdrawn. Some may even begin to harbor thoughts of suicide.[1]

Another major health problem in the United States today is the result of increased cocaine use. An estimated ten to twenty million persons are regular users, with an additional five thousand trying cocaine for the first time every year. Many suffer severe health effects and have to seek treatment eventually. The number of emergency room visits for cocaine-related conditions actually tripled in the years from 1983 to 1987. And the number of deaths as a result of cocaine abuse is running at close to six hundred a year.[2]

The main effects of cocaine on the human body are a faster heartbeat and a jump in blood pressure. Nausea and vomiting may be present. Some people have hallucinations. Many complain of sleeping disorders. Mental confusion is another frequent symptom.

Long-time cocaine abusers fall victim to additional problems. Because cocaine is usually sniffed through the nose, the mucous membrane becomes sore and tender. At first the only problem is a runny nose. Later, there are perforations in the nasal septum that may require surgery to repair.

Cold sweats, convulsions, fainting, and breathing difficulties also appear in heavy abusers. And deaths due to cardiac arrest, stroke, or respiratory failure are not at all uncommon.

One especially uncomfortable result of cocaine addiction is a condition called formication or "cocaine bugs." Victims believe that snakes and insects are crawling on their skin and digging into their bodies. They scratch until they bleed to get rid of these imaginary bugs.

Cocaine use quickly leads to a strong dependency. In 1986, 25,700 cocaine users were in treatment. Researchers estimate, though, that of that number nearly 17,000 will return to cocaine after their discharge.

Amphetamines also stimulate the central nervous system, giving the user a quick burst of energy. But while the effects of cocaine last only for a few minutes, the high from amphetamines lasts hours. After a few hours of a racing heartbeat and high blood pressure, though, feelings of fatigue, nervousness, irritability, and a general depression take over. Heavy abusers sometimes become paranoid, convinced that people are out to harm or even kill them. Weight loss and chest pains also develop with long-time use.[3]

Heroin, the favorite narcotic of American drug abusers, has a number of possible bad effects. The first time someone injects heroin, the usual reaction is strong nausea. Gradually, the drug user overcomes this feeling, but with continued use come more serious health problems. These include difficulty in sleeping, blacking out for periods of time, loss of weight, malnutrition, and respiratory disease.

Heavy users of heroin suffer severe withdrawal symptoms when they try to stop. The addict usually shakes uncontrollably and may go into convulsions. Aches and cramps are commonly accompanied by sharp pains, chills, and sweating.

Large doses of heroin cause users to fall into a very deep sleep. Their skin becomes cold, moist, and bluish in color. Breathing slows down. In the worst cases, death caused by shock or respiratory failure sometimes follows.

A further set of perils is connected with the needles used to inject the heroin. The veins used for repeated injection can collapse. The person can develop infections and abscesses at the points of injection, some of which may prove to be fatal. If the needles are not clean, there is a chance of developing blood poisoning or hepatitis.

Also, as was mentioned earlier, the AIDS virus can be passed from one addict to another when sharing a contaminated needle. AIDS is, right now, a disease without a cure. And, by weakening a person's immune system and ability to fight off disease, the virus infection almost always results in early death.[4]

When PCP, or angel dust, was first synthesized in 1957 it was promoted as an anesthetic for animals. It was not until 1967 that it made its way into the drug world, where it quickly became one of the most popular—and potent—of the hallucinogenic drugs.

Abusers choose PCP for making them feel drunk in a way they enjoy—happy, no worries, highly sensitive to everything going on around them, and free of all their usual concerns. But these same abusers also suffer the side effects of a bad PCP trip—terrifying hallucinations, a distorted perception of reality, bizarre actions, mental confusion, a tendency to violent behavior, and great fear and anxiety.

After heavy, continued abuse of PCP, the results can be much worse—permanent loss of a sense of reality, convulsions, and respiratory failure, followed by coma and death.[5]

PERSONALITY CHANGES

Drug users usually think that they can handle drugs better than they really can. They feel sure that they can have a safe high and suffer no bad reactions. Also, few will admit that they have lost control and cannot stop their drug use.

Few beginning users notice how drugs affect their personality or twist their thoughts. Drugs make users deny the truth. Some say that they are taking less of the stuff than they really are. Or they claim to be using drugs less often than is the case.

Most users convince themselves that drugs are basically harmless and that they will never develop a drug habit. As one former addict recounted, "Almost everybody says, 'Oh, I can stop if I want to. It's not that I need it. It's just a good time. This is no problem. I just do it 'cause I like it.' "

Most experts agree that the problem is one of denial. "You can lie to yourself for the rest of your life if you want to," the former addict continues. "But you're not fooling anybody else. So for people that are the least bit weak in terms of being able to go their own way, it's extremely dangerous."

Tests show that drugs interfere with mental ability. Drugs can also cause the user to have lower grades in school or perform poorly on the job. Students on drugs often get into trouble with teachers and principals; employees pick fights with other workers and suffer increased tension and anxiety. Some kids even have to drop out of school; adults may lose their jobs and fail in their careers.

One heavy user of marijuana spoke about how his personality changed: "My high school went down the drain. I think I would have been quite a few years ahead if I didn't take drugs. I probably would have been in college now. I think my attention span has decreased. When I'm high on marijuana, my attention span is that of a five year old."

"Pot totally kills your motivation, that's what I think," said one teenaged marijuana smoker. "You're unmotivated to do anything."

A 1983 Gallup survey of teenagers showed that 35 percent considered drug abuse a "very big" school problem and 23 percent a "fairly big" one. Over one-third called drug abuse "the biggest problem facing their generation."[6]

Drug use also makes it harder to get along with others. Users are jumpy and irritable. They argue more with their parents and brothers and sisters. Also, they pressure friends to start doing drugs. Trying to get friends to change their ways often leads to fights and breaks up friendships. Drug users find it hard to decide between right and wrong. Paranoia and aggression also tend to go along with cocaine and crack use.

DRUGS AND SUICIDE

In March 1987, four New Jersey teenagers were killed in a car crash. The autopsies showed that they had been taking cocaine. The experts think that they had gotten high on the drug. Then, when the effects wore off, they went into a deep depression. They felt that life was not worth living. And so they made a suicide pact and took their own lives.

At least 5,200 youths between the ages of fifteen and twenty-four commit suicide every year. And there is little doubt of the relation between depressants such as heroin, barbiturates, and alcohol and an increased risk of suicide.

The cycle goes something like this: People who are depressed take drugs like heroin to make themselves feel better. They seem to enjoy better mental health for a while but then grow even more unhappy than before. To combat these deeper feelings of despair they step up their drug use.[7]

In Britain, as an example, about twenty times more heroin addicts kill themselves than members of the general population.

Drugs that lead to confusion and depression may also result in recklessness. In fact, some deaths involving drugs are ruled accidental on the assumption that the victim simply didn't know—or didn't care—how much of the drug he or she was taking.

Driving after smoking marijuana is a frequent cause of accidental death. One nineteen-year-old gave this disconnected account of his marijuana-related accident: "And then I saw a teacup on the road . . . real cup and saucer. Pink with blue flowers. Like in home . . . on road in front of me . . . six people in it . . . just sitting there, riding down the road. We were behind it . . . I was going to crash into it . . . went off the road."

The turn-of-the-century French sociologist, Emile Durkheim, stated his theory of suicide. He said that too little guidance and too much separation from society made people consider killing themselves. Many modern experts believe that these same two factors are also important in leading to drug abuse. Thus, suicide and drug abuse may be linked in this way. They are both reactions to the same difficulties.[8]

Also, there are psychological similarities between drug abusers and teens who commit suicide. People argue about which comes first—drug abuse or the psychological factors that lead to it. But almost everyone agrees that drug abuse can cause suicidal behavior because of the way it affects the mind and body and the way it affects personal and social attitudes.

Health damage, personality changes, increased suicide—these are a part of the terrible toll drug abuse takes day by day on the health and well-being of millions in our society.

5
AIDS

Laura is twenty-six years old and a high school dropout. She works in a beauty parlor. Although she experimented with drugs for a few years, neither she nor her present boyfriend uses drugs.

Last year, when Laura went for her regular checkup, her doctor discovered that she was infected with the AIDS virus. Laura broke down and sobbed. Right away she realized that she had contracted the virus during the time she lived with a man named Joe. Joe never took the trouble to sterilize the needles he used to shoot up heroin. His desire to have the drug was always too urgent.

About two months after learning that she had AIDS, Laura got another piece of shocking news. She was pregnant. The first question she asked the doctor was: "Will my baby have AIDS?" She was told that the chances were about fifty-fifty.

In time, Laura did have her baby, a little girl whom she named Lisa. The doctors could not tell whether or not Lisa had the disease. It would take about a year before they could be sure.

Yet Lisa was a sickly child. She cried a lot and did not grow and gain weight as fast as she should have. Caring for her was very difficult. The baby demanded a lot of care and attention. No babysitters stayed long enough for Laura to return to work.

Soon Laura gave up trying to care for her baby. She placed the infant in a foster home because she was afraid the baby was sick and would soon die. As for telling the man she lived with that she had AIDS—she didn't. If he left her, she thought, life would be too lonely.

Laura is not yet showing any symptoms of the disease. But she knows that things will soon get much worse. There is a good chance that she has infected her boyfriend with the disease. Sooner or later she, her child, and the man she loves will probably get very sick and die.

Unfortunately, this tragedy is occurring over and over again. Someone carrying the AIDS virus uses a needle to shoot up heroin. Some of the viruses get onto the needle. Another person uses the same needle. The viruses get into his or her system.

The infected individual has sex with someone else. Through the mingling of body fluids, the virus infects the partner. When a woman infected with the virus gets pregnant, the germs can pass over into the fetus. Often the baby is born with the virus.

THE STORY OF AIDS

In June 1981 reports from New York City in the East and Los Angeles in the West told of pneumonia patients whose immune systems had ceased to function. Because the problem concerned the immune system—the part of the body that fights invading diseases—the doctors called this condition Acquired Immune Deficiency Syndrome, or AIDS. In time researchers learned that AIDS is caused by a virus. They called it HIV, short for human immunosuppressive virus.

Although AIDS was not recognized as a disease until 1981, it is believed that the virus first came to the United States around 1977. The virus is known to have caused trouble in areas near the equator in Africa in the early 1970s, with equal numbers of men and women showing symptoms of what we now call AIDS.

Some of the people infected were Haitians who had spent time in Africa from 1960 to the mid-1970s. These individuals returned to their island nation in the Caribbean and brought the disease with them.

According to one theory, the AIDS virus was first brought to the United States by a Canadian air steward named Gaetan Dugas. Dugas is believed to have contracted the disease through sexual contacts with Africans. Of the first nineteen cases of AIDS reported in Los Angeles, eight were linked to Dugas or one of his sex partners.

The AIDS virus, many others believe, came to the United States by way of refugees or travelers from Haiti; a number of infected Haitian prostitutes made their way here, for example. And there were also some homosexual men from the United States who had gone to Haiti, picked up the virus there, and carried it back with them.

The situation changed in December 1982. That is when the first case of AIDS possibly related to blood transfusions was reported. People were afraid that the nation's blood supply might be contaminated with the AIDS virus.

Slowly, but steadily, the disease spread. By the beginning of 1983 it became clear that AIDS could be transmitted to and by women. They could pick up the virus from a sexual partner and pass it on to another. And a pregnant woman with AIDS could give the disease to her baby.

Next, AIDS began to appear among IV drug users. Drug users sharing contaminated needles sent the number of AIDS cases way up. In New York City, the proportion of IV drug abusers who have developed AIDS has increased dramatically. They made up 22 percent of the AIDS cases in 1981. By 1986, the figure had risen to a staggering 36 percent. At this time, 50 to 60 percent of the city's 200,000 heroin addicts are believed to be infected with the HIV virus.[1]

THE EFFECTS OF AIDS

A person suffering the symptoms of AIDS is in the final stages of the disease. But the disease can be detected before any signs appear.

When the virus enters the blood stream it attacks certain white blood cells. The body begins to produce certain substances, called antibodies, to fight the viruses. These antibodies can be detected in the blood by a simple test. If a person is infected with AIDS, the test for the HIV antibodies will be positive.

The AIDS virus itself does not kill. But it can produce such symptoms as extreme tiredness, rapid weight loss, swollen lymph glands, white spots in the mouth, persistent dry cough, diarrhea, and skin blotches or bumps on the skin that vary from blue-violet to brown in color.

The HIV attacks the immune system. With the immune system not functioning properly, the patient is open to diseases that would not bother a normally healthy person. The long list of illnesses that can move in are called opportunistic diseases. Among these, the most important ones are a type of pneumonia known as PCP or PC, and a form of cancer known as Kaposis sarcoma.

The AIDS sickness can follow several different courses. Some people remain well but can infect others. Others develop a less serious disease than AIDS, which has the name AIDS Related Complex (ARC). And some develop AIDS.

Right now there are dozens of laboratories studying

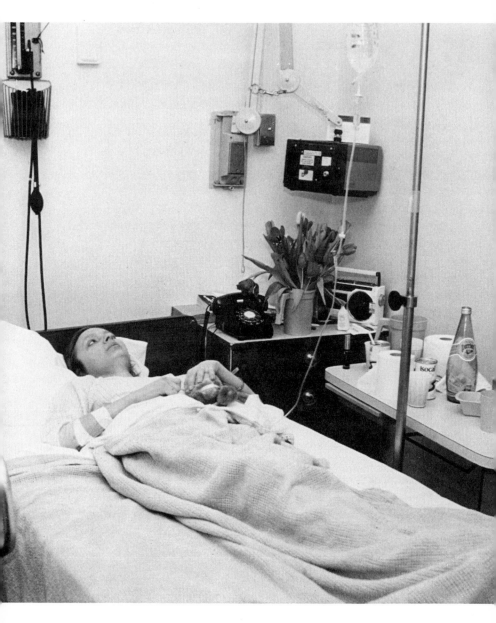

*A young woman ill with AIDS is
being treated in a hospital.*

AIDS. All are seeking ways to prevent, control, or cure the disease. Although the scientists are learning more about the condition every day, there's still a lot they don't know. Most of the current treatment methods focus on the secondary illnesses. Doctors, for example, often prescribe interferon for those with Kaposis sarcoma. Surgery, radiation, and such drugs as Interleukin-2 hold some promise for some of the other conditions.

CHILDREN WITH AIDS

Almost every child with AIDS was born to a mother who was a carrier of the virus. Only a very few get the disease from a contaminated blood transfusion. Pregnant women with the AIDS virus have an even chance of passing it on to their children. Seventy-eight percent of all children with AIDS are actually born with the disease.

Most scientists believe that babies can acquire AIDS while still in the womb of an infected mother. They can also get AIDS while passing through the birth canal during the birth process. Certain experts believe that the virus can even pass to the baby from the milk of an infected mother.

Doctors say it is difficult to diagnose children under one year of age for the AIDS virus antibodies. The tests are inconclusive because infants whose mothers are infected inherit virus antibodies whether or not they carry the virus itself. For that reason doctors are looking for ways to identify infected children quickly and begin treatment early. One approach that is being studied is to look for a difference in the shape of the newborn's face. If this proves to be a good diagnostic tool, it will suggest that the fetus was infected between the twelfth and sixteenth week of gestation.[2]

By and large, children with AIDS do not live beyond their third birthday. A recent report by the Citizens' Committee for Children warned of an "ominously rising tide" of AIDS and AIDS-related illnesses in children.

Nationwide, more than two thousand children are thought to have either AIDS or AIDS-related illnesses. Forty percent of them are in New York City. These children, most of them infected before birth, are usually born to the poorest families, where more and more women carry the virus due to drug abuse or sexual contact with drug abusers. In New York City, eight of ten children with AIDS have drug-abusing parents, and nine of ten are black or Hispanic.[3]

AIDS takes a terrible toll on its young victims. One of the first children ever diagnosed with AIDS is now nine and a half years old. She is the size of a six year old and walks and talks haltingly, because of brain damage due to the AIDS virus. A recent study of six- to eight-year-old children with AIDS showed that nearly 90 percent had similar nervous-system problems.[4]

A seven-year-old boy's face is round and puffy from the medicines he takes. His blood platelet count is so low that his hands swell and discolor if he does something as simple as punching a rubber ball.

Another boy, age six and a half, was abandoned by his drug-abusing parents and spent his first five years in a hospital. Now he is emotionally disturbed and is often separated from other children because of unruly behavior.

One six-year-old girl struggles to breathe because of her AIDS-damaged lungs. Sometimes she must stop playing to rest in a wheelchair. As with many other children with AIDS, her neck is thick with chronically swollen lymph glands and her fingers are wide and clubbed at the tips.

Children with AIDS suffer the many different symptoms of the disease. But they must also endure the fear and isolation caused by the unreasonable fear of AIDS in the general population. Many children and babies, known as "boarder babies," live in so-called boarder homes because their parents cannot or will not care for them. Certain school boards don't let children who carry the AIDS virus attend school. Some parents don't let them play with their children. Even doctors and nurses sometimes refuse to treat them out of fear of contracting the disease.

Dr. James M. Oleske, a pediatrician at the University of Medicine and Dentistry of New Jersey, says that children with AIDS often have fever, anemia, and diarrhea. They tend to be passive and show a lack of interest in living. About half have cardiovascular abnormalities and some type of pneumonia. Neurological problems also occur, causing seizures and spasms and, in rare cases, making the victims blind, mute, or deaf.

AIDS IN THE COMMUNITY

Some startling figures came out at a conference on AIDS sponsored by the Centers for Disease Control in Atlanta, Georgia, in August 1987. Blacks and Hispanics make up 19 percent of the total population, yet they account for 38 percent of all reported cases of AIDS— exactly twice as many as would be expected! The figures for children are even worse. Eighty percent of all youngsters with AIDS are either black or Hispanic!

The statistics also tell us that AIDS, which started off as a disease of Africans, Haitians, homosexuals, and IV drug abusers, is now more widespread among drug users than previously believed. This trend has very serious ramifications for American society.

First and foremost, it is a tragic waste of human lives. By May 1988, 60,852 AIDS cases had occurred nationwide, according to the Centers for Disease Control. In New York City alone, 53 percent of all AIDS-related deaths, since the epidemic began, involve intravenous drug users. Drug addicts are thought to pose a greater threat to the general population than homosexuals.

AIDS may already have impacted our economy more than we realize. Sales of diagnostic blood tests for the AIDS virus exceeded $150 million in 1986. And medical costs, including nursing care for AIDS patients, are estimated to average $125,000. Drug companies are spending millions in the search for new drugs, and the Federal government alone spent $200 million in 1986 for AIDS research.

The cost to American life insurance companies of AIDS-related deaths could reach $50 billion by the year 2000, according to an industry study.[5] The insurance industry, which does not now offer life and health policies for drug addicts, now wants to exclude AIDS patients. "Anyone who would test positive for the virus would be uninsurable," says a representative of Nationwide Insurance Company. Many feel that this kind of action is discriminatory and denies AIDS patients the same rights as other ill people. Three states—California, Florida, and Wisconsin—have already acted to forbid insurance companies to pursue this practice.

Nevertheless, America is devoting many resources to the search for an AIDS cure. But will this interest and flow of money continue once it becomes identified as a ghetto or minority disease? Many think not. "In the heroin crisis of the late 1960s and again with crack in recent years it was the threat to the middle- and upper-middle-class kids that put pressure on legislatures and Congress," said Dr. Mitchell S. Rosenthal, president of Phoenix House, the drug treatment centers in New York and California. "There is a danger that if they feel less of a threat, the resources won't stay with the problem."

Also, there is the question of how the poor communities will react to seeing AIDS spreading and killing their population. Some fear that it will unleash an even greater wave of drug abuse. Dr. Beny J. Primm, executive director of the Addiction Research and Treatment Corporation, has given his vision of the future in the country's poorest neighborhoods. "Five years from now, those people who are alive then will find their ranks devastated by AIDS, and there will be a type of hopelessness that is hard to imagine now. I am hearing people already say, 'I am infected with the virus, I might as well shoot up drugs.' People will be turning more and more to drugs for solace."[6]

AIDS is already a serious menace to our society and the worst is yet to come. Federal experts estimate that by 1991, 270,000 men and women will be infected by the virus and 179,000 of them will die. The only hope for our society and the only way to avoid this catastrophe is to redouble our efforts to find a cure and way of treating the disease.

STREET CRIME

The young man is walking down the supermarket aisle. He seems to have plenty of time and not know what to buy. At the end of one aisle a mother is kneeling over tying the shoelaces of her two-year-old son. The man glances around and starts walking more quickly. As he passes the mother and child, he yanks the purse off the woman's lap.

She starts to run after him, shouting, "Stop him! Stop the thief!"

Rushing out of his office, the supermarket manager is able to grab the fleeing man. While the two men are fighting, the thief whips out a switchblade knife and slashes the manager's hand. A couple of people wrestle the attacker to the ground and hold him there while someone calls the police.

Within minutes a patrol car pulls up to the store. An officer handcuffs the young man and drives him to the station house. While frisking him for weapons, the police find two joints of marijuana and a dozen vials of crack. The police book him for robbery and possession of illegal drugs.

Two girls are lurking in the dark shadows just outside the movie theater parking lot. They are chatting, but their eyes are scanning the many cars arriving for the evening show. After a while, the cars stop pulling in. The parking lot grows quiet, filled with autos.

The young women step out of the shadows and move toward a shiny new sports car parked off to one side. One girl reaches into her backpack and pulls out a long, shiny metal device. Working quietly and surely she plunges it between the window glass and the metal of the door. She gives a sharp upward pull and the door pops open.

Without wasting a motion, the girls slide into the front seat, take out a handful of tools and start removing the car's expensive radio and tape deck. In a few minutes, they pull out the components and unplug the trailing wires.

Gently placing the equipment in the backpack, they open the door and step out. To their horror, they walk into the arms of a couple of waiting cops.

"Just what do you think you're doing?" one says as they hustle the girls into the patrol car.

At the station, someone notices the girls' arms, covered with small red marks, some of which even seem to be infected.

"Been shooting heroin?" an officer asks.

"None of your damned business," comes the reply.

"I'm afraid it is, I'm afraid it is," says the policeman sadly shaking his head from side to side.

Most Americans' fear of crime is at a very high level. People generally believe that the desire for drugs is creating crime waves that are making them feel unsafe in the streets or even in their homes. Drug abuse is considered one of the most important urban problems. In the words of Benjamin Ward, Police Commissioner of New York City, "The crime problem in America today *is* the drug problem."[1]

INCIDENCE OF
DRUG-RELATED CRIME

Many people agree that there is a close connection between street crime and drug abuse. Some experts estimate that as many as 100 million crimes a year are committed by drug abusers. They also say that narcotics addicts alone are responsible for about half of these criminal acts.

A 1986 study showed how crime is fueled by drug abuse. In New York and Washington, researchers found that 56 percent of all criminal suspects tested were using drugs at the time of arrest. In Florida as cocaine arrests rose 80 percent, the burglary rate went up 30 percent. The city of Bridgeport, Connecticut, reported thirty murders in 1985 and forty-one in 1986. The authorities are convinced that drug abuse was largely responsible for the increase.[2]

The number of murders in New York City went up 20 percent from 1985 to 1986. According to the Citizens Crime Commission, most of the rise could be blamed on the growing use of crack and other drugs.

Crimes committed by drug abusers, it is said, show the relaxed attitude people in the drug culture have toward the law. The attitude seems to be that if you are breaking one law, you might as well break another. Or it may be that the high cost of drugs combined with the difficulty in getting and holding a job gives drug abusers few options on how to get money.

But there are those who believe that the drug-crime link is exaggerated. The question is: Do drug users turn to a life of crime to support their drug habits? Or do drugs worsen existing criminal careers?

The argument calls for some very careful consideration.

DRUGS AND CRIME:
CAUSE OR EFFECT?

During the 1950s, heroin addiction remained at low levels in white neighborhoods. But it grew at an alarming rate among the youths of black America and other minority populations. For many of the disadvantaged, drug use became a way of life. And street crime was typically part of their drug-taking and drug-seeking activities. Most people, at that time, assumed that drug abuse led to crime. The reasoning seemed to make perfect sense: Drug abuse is a very expensive habit. Very few people have enough money to pay for daily drug use. One of the most obvious ways to obtain more money for drugs is through crime.

The first question of whether there is a direct, cause/effect connection between drugs and crime came in the 1967 report of the President's Commission on Law Enforcement and Administration of Justice. It said: "The simple truth is that the extent of the addict's or drug abuser's responsibility for all nondrug offenses is unknown . . . but there is no reliable data to assess properly the common assertion that drug users or addicts are responsible for 50 percent of all crime."[3]

The NIDA has funded a number of studies to collect basic information on the drug-crime connection. Here are a few of the conclusions:[4]

The number of crimes committed by drug abusers is higher than previously believed.

All addicts commit crime by virtue of the fact that they use illegal drugs. But narcotics users are involved more often, with more different kinds of crimes, and with more violence than nonnarcotics users.

Heroin users commit more crimes when they are taking the drug than when they are not on the drug.

Whether or not heroin turns law-abiding citizens into criminals is uncertain. One study found that people arrested for narcotics-law violations also tend to have criminal records that date back to before their first narcotic arrest.

A great number of heroin users are actually career offenders. Early on, they adopted criminality as a way of life. Addicts are, on average, less than fifteen years old at the time of their first crime. But they generally don't start doing heroin until they are nearly nineteen. Many were already on the wrong side of the law before they got hooked on drugs. As a result, the high proportion of heroin-addict crime may be unrelated to their drug abuse.

What about the idea that the high cost of maintaining a heroin habit leads to crime? As is generally known, heroin addicts find it difficult to hold steady, legitimate jobs. Also, their powerful need to seek and find heroin every six hours takes up much of their time and energy. And arrests and other entanglements with the law frequently add to their money troubles. This would seem to suggest that crime follows the need to support an addiction to narcotics.

But some recent research suggests another view. While narcotics use intensifies and perpetuates criminal careers, it may not start them. As James Inciardi points out in his study, *The War on Drugs*: "Narcotics use freezes its users into patterns of criminality that are more acute, dynamic, violent, unremitting, and enduring than those of other drug-using offenders."[5]

To support his argument, Inciardi cites a Miami study that included 573 narcotics users and 429 whose drug use did not include narcotics. Primarily this group used alcohol, sedatives, marijuana, and/or cocaine. Compared to the heroin users, the nonnarcotic drug users reported fewer crimes per person. Also, their crimes were not quite as serious. Almost two-thirds of the crimes had to do with shoplifting, prostitution, and drug sales compared to the narcotics-using groups, which had significantly larger proportions of the more serious crimes of robbery and burglary.

From 1977 through 1985, a number of investigators interviewed in one study more than 3,000 drug users to learn even more about criminal activity in the drug community. Of the 387 men and 186 women interviewed, 99.5 percent admitted they had committed crimes in the last year, 92.5 percent had an arrest history, and 77.8 percent had served time in prison. Together they had been involved in over 215,000 criminal acts. That works out to an average of 375 crimes per person per year![6]

The most frequent types of crimes were: dealing in drugs (82,449), prostitution (26,045), shoplifting (25,045), possessing stolen goods (17,240), and gambling (12,939). Other high-rate crimes were forgery (7,504), procuring for prostitutes (7,107), burglary (6,669), theft (6,668) and robbery (5,300). Included in the list, but with less frequent occurrence, are assault, auto theft, pickpocketing, arson, vandalism, fraud, extortion, and loan-sharking.[7]

Although these figures are very high, some experts say that they are not as bad as they seem. Some 60 percent of the total are so-called victimless crimes. The main crimes of this sort are drug dealing, prostitution, gambling, and procuring.

New trends show a shift from heroin to crack abuse in inner-city neighborhoods. Some law enforcement officials say that the transition from heroin to crack may lead to an increase in the rate of violent crimes.

DRUGS AND VIOLENCE

In early winter of 1987, a New York City man apparently on crack held four people hostage for thirty hours in a New York City apartment. Armed with a gun, the man demanded baking soda from the police, which they feared he would use to change powdered cocaine into smokable crack.[8]

Since crack use has become widespread, police and drug treatment experts have reported an increasing number of cases of violent, erratic, and bizarre behavior among heavy cocaine users. The symptoms are said to be similar to schizophrenia and other severe psychotic disorders. In one case, a patient told the psychiatrist that he was able to jump from building top to building top. Another patient ran into a liquor store claiming he was being chased by a mad dog. Someone else knocked down an apartment door because he believed that a mob was following him.

As the use of crack spreads in the inner city, police are reporting rising numbers of murders and violent, unpredictable behavior among drug abusers. Says Deputy Chief Francis Hall, head of the New York City Police Department's narcotics division, "The escalated use of cocaine has truly changed the drug problem. Heroin maintained people on an even keel, it was sort of a tranquilizer. Cocaine causes a very different reaction."[9]

Dr. Jochanan Weisenfreund, psychiatrist, agrees. "By comparison, heroin addicts were pussycats," he says. "In my opinion, the police should approach a crack addict as they would approach someone with acute psychiatric disorder."[10]

Police in Florida have noticed an increase in burglaries and armed robberies in areas where crack is sold. Says Captain Robert Lamont of the Dade County police narcotics division, "These are the crimes that generate enough cash for a quick fix. Then it's off to the streets to raise more cash."[11] The world of crack is said to be built on violence. The base houses where crack is sold and smoked are built like fortresses and they are protected by tight security to ward off police and competitors.

A cocaine habit costs a hundred dollars or more every week. To get this much money, people often do things that are unethical or illegal. As cocaine use has grown among middle-class men and women, there has been a steady rise in nonviolent and white-collar crime. Borrowing money from banks, businesses, friends, and families and not repaying it is frequent. Shoplifting, credit-card scams, prostitution, passing bad checks, embezzlement, and theft of goods for resale is also common. Another type of crime involves stealing money or jewelry from friends or family.

Some drug abusers find that they can get their daily supply without money. They barter. The *New York Times* tells how middle-class cocaine abusers exchange their skills and services for cocaine. Carpenters and plumbers often fix up rooms in abandoned buildings for the dealers' headquarters. But instead of being paid money for their work, they get payment in the form of drugs from the dealers. Some lawyers and doctors carry this even further. They get paid in drugs—and then turn around and sell the drugs for money!

Paul J. Goldstein, of Narcotic and Drug Research, Inc., presented a paper entitled "Drugs and Violent Behavior," at the Annual Meeting of the Academy of Criminal Justice Sciences on April 28, 1982. In it he described three causes of violence among drug abusers. One is the commonly accepted idea that addicts commit crimes to pay for their habit. Goldstein calls this the "economically compulsive model of violence."[12]

Many heroin and cocaine users fit this model. Over a third engage in violent crimes, often committing robberies with a gun to get money for their drugs. Among the women, prostitution is listed as the most frequently committed crime. But the researchers found that prostitution did not produce very much income. To get enough money for their drug habit, the women also turned to assaulting and robbing their customers, as well as to shoplifting.

Goldstein's second point is that doing drugs is an illegal activity. Therefore, everyone involved in drugs is on the wrong side of the law. On this basis, then, it is very easy to fall into a life of crime. In Goldstein's words, this is the "systemic model of violence."[13]

And finally there are some people who react to the drugs they are taking by becoming violent or antisocial. In these cases it is the drugs themselves that cause the criminal behavior. Goldstein labels this the "psychopharmacological model of violence."[14]

Researchers have found that certain substances cause hostile acts more than others. The level of violence depends on a number of factors: the specific drug, the dosage, the time and place of the drug use, the established pattern for conduct under that drug, and the user's mood and personality.

Drug reactions take a number of different paths. Stimulants, such as cocaine and amphetamines, give a sudden burst of energy, cause impulsive behavior, and create a paranoid suspicion of others—all of which can lead to violence. Amphetamines are more likely to be involved in senseless, aggressive crime than cocaine. Delusions, loss of control, and repetitive motor acts, such as continuing to stab or club a victim long dead, can result in bizarre crimes without obvious motivation.

Hallucinogens, like PCP and LSD, can be responsible for some outrageous acts of violence. The combination of delusion of power, insensitivity to the pain of others, no memory for the past, and poor self-control can have horrible outcomes. A sense of bravado or omnipotence results in an absence of care and caution.

Barbiturate users tend to be unpredictable, uncoordinated, and usually confused. They may become overactive, hostile, nasty, and irritable. The drug can quench their fears and give them the courage to carry out robberies and other criminal acts.

In studies of drug-using prisoners, many of those convicted of aggravated assault, robbery, and burglary, were abusers of barbiturates. One researcher found that barbiturate users had the highest rate of violent crimes compared with other drug users. Motorcycle gang members are known to prefer barbiturates or other tranquilizers before getting into a street fight.

Narcotics, such as opium and morphine, as stated previously, are associated with mostly nonviolent crimes, such as shoplifting, prostitution, drug dealing, and theft. But in recent years armed robbery, burglary, and assault have become more frequent among narcotics abusers. Rolling drunks, that is, going through the victim's pockets while he is intoxicated or sleeping, is the specialty of some junkies.

PROSTITUTION

Since the 1860s, many investigators have accepted a link between female drug users and prostitution. As Bingham Dai wrote in his study of drug addiction in Chicago in the 1930s: "That the pimp in his attempt to entice a girl to his service [as a prostitute] not seldom 'dopes' her and makes her an addict so that she will have to depend on him for her drug and thereby becomes his woman is a matter of common knowledge."[15]

Marsha Rosenbaum, in her 1981 book, *Women On Heroin*, reaches a similar conclusion: "Initial and short-range heroin use is generally not costly to women, but ultimately she must begin to support her heroin habit and generally resorts to illegal means to do so."[16]

Recent findings suggest new conclusions on the drugs-prostitution connection. Some now hold that there is no evidence either that prostitution causes narcotic dependence or that narcotic dependence leads to prostitution. Others indicate that prostitutes use drugs as much as other groups on the outskirts of society.

An analysis of 397 women who were using drugs and had engaged in prostitution provides the following insights: About three-quarters had histories of current or past heroin use, while the remaining women were nonheroin users. Heroin users had a history of criminality before their involvement with the drug.

Female heroin users tend primarily to be drug dealers because selling is a relatively easy and safe economic pursuit. Prostitution usually begins only after some disruption in the women's drug-dealing activities, usually not being able to obtain a regular supply of heroin. The women remain prostitutes after that.

Drug use in prostitutes on heroin, as with other addicts, is a criminal career. But this involvement with drugs may not necessarily lead to activities such as stealing and dealing. What the facts almost surely show is this: Where present, heroin use in prostitutes intensifies a life of crime and keeps it going.

AIDS SCARE AND CRIME

For a while, the most-wanted bank robber in New York used the same technique. He handed the teller a note that read: "I'm dying of AIDS. I don't give a —— and will shoot you if you try anything stupid. Give me all your 100, 50, 20, 10 dollar bills." Most of the times he got what he asked for.

The frequency of the robberies led detectives of the New York Police Department to believe that the man was supplying his drug habit. And based on the physical description of witnesses, who said that he seemed to be losing weight, investigators assumed that he had AIDS. As it turned out, they were right on both counts.

In 1985, Paul J. Goldstein commented on the connection between drugs, AIDS, and crime: "The current AIDS scare has led to an increasing amount of violence because of intravenous drug-users' fear of contracting this fatal disease from contaminated 'works' [needles and syringes used in some drug-taking]."[17] Some sellers of needles and syringes claim that the used works they are offering for sale are actually new and unused. If found out by would-be purchasers, violence may ensue.

A recent incident led to the death of two men. A heroin user kept a set of works in a "shooting gallery" for his exclusive use. One day another man used these works. The owner of the works discovered what had happened and stabbed the borrower to death. The murderer later fatally wounded a friend who was present when the stranger had used the works, had done nothing to stop him, and had failed to inform the owner of what had happened.

Statistically, the persons most likely to harm or be harmed by drugs are those who have had the most difficulty advancing in modern American society. These are mostly big-city, slum-dwelling males, usually from minority groups. These groups are also overrepresented in the commission of crimes in the street and in arrests.

Obviously, crime is a terrible burden and blot on our society. It causes great pain and loss and even death to the victims and can often ruin the lives of the criminals. Although the exact connection between drugs and crime is not yet established, there is ample proof that the connection does exist. Thus, preventing drug abuse is one way of improving the quality of life for everyone.

DRUG DEALING

The city block where Mario lives is a wide-open drug market. Dealers with gold chains around their necks and telephone beepers on their hips line the sidewalks. Residents of the block sit or stand in doorways smoking crack. Inside the deserted, boarded-up buildings, addicts shoot heroin. Now and then, a suburbanite or student-type stops his or her car and makes a drug purchase.

Not long ago two hundred police officers swarmed into Mario's block. They made a clean sweep of the entire street, end to end. Dozens of people were arrested and several apartments were raided. Police patrols continued for several weeks. Every day, people were rounded up and booked on narcotics charges.

As a result, the amount of drug activity on the street went way down. But the improvement didn't last very long. Soon the dealers, the "cockroaches," as they are called, were back. Mario was not really surprised. He says the appetite for drugs and the profits from dealing are so great that nothing will stop the illegal sale of drugs.

In a way, Mario's street is typical of thousands of others in cities and towns all over America inhabited by victims of drug abuse. Those who lose most, of course, are the ones who use and trade drugs right on these streets. Tragedy in many different forms stalks their lives, from sickness to early death, from shattered dreams to years in prison.

Although the drug dealers make huge amounts of money, they also suffer. Most often they themselves are addicts and spend most of their profits on their own drug needs. Their lives are filled with constant fear—of the police, of thieves trying to steal their money or drug supply, of rival dealers attempting to take over their territory, of angry or crazed addicts, and of decent residents working to drive them off the street.

But everyone else on the block pays a price, too. Parents suffer as they watch their children being seduced by the allures of drug use and dealing. The merchants can't do business because customers are afraid to walk on the drug-dealing streets. Innocent bystanders are injured or killed in the violent wars between drug lords. And homelessness and rootlessness result as nondrug users flee the block, abandoning homes and stores to addicts and dealers.

DRUGS AND DOLLARS

Drugs are big business. In fact, the *New York Times* reports that "drug-abusing Americans pay perhaps $110 billion a year for their habit."[1]

The Treasury Department gives a few instances of the huge sums of money involved in the drug trade:[2]

• New York City: Federal agents arrest twelve drug traffickers. They seize 11,600 pounds (5,300 kg) of hashish, 1.5 pounds (.7 kg) of Thai sticks, and 5,000 units of LSD. But, in addition, the agents find $400,000 in cash, a painting worth one million dollars, jewelry valued at $100,000, and a new Mercedes automobile.

- San Francisco: Federal agents arrest two drug traffickers. They seize 23.5 pounds (11 kg) of cocaine. But, in addition, the agents find a bank account with a balance of $212,000, stocks worth $15,000, and the deed to a $750,000 house.
- Miami: Federal agents arrest a man who helped to finance drug operations. They seize 44 pounds (20 kg) of pure cocaine. But, in addition, the agents find one million dollars in cash and a number of secret Swiss bank accounts.
- Scranton, Pennsylvania: Federal agents arrest five members of a drug ring. They don't find any drugs, but they dig up over $4 million in $20 bills buried near the home of the operation's leader.

The people involved in America's drug trade form a sort of pyramid. At the top are the drug lords, the operators of big drug rings who furnish the capital for these businesses. A number of the top drug lords are actually billionaires from money they've made in the drug trade. Some of them operate behind fancy—but false—corporate facades. They live very well, in neighborhoods with other high-income business people and wealthy professionals. Active in PTA or local church groups, they contribute generously to community causes.

When asked what they do for a living they are always vague:

"I own a trading corporation."

"What do you trade?"

"Oh, various items."

"Where do you sell them?"

"Here and abroad."

Beneath the top bosses are the distributors. Each distributor controls one area or one city. They are, in effect, drug wholesalers. For example, one distributor provides all the heroin that a certain crime family sells in Chicago. Another individual is the source of all the cocaine in Dallas. And so on. The profits in the drug trade are so huge that the distributors are paid very generously for their work.

The runners are below the distributors on the drug-dealing pyramid. These people bring the drugs to America from South America, Asia, and the Middle East. Some runners are pilots who fly in shipments of drugs; they are sometimes paid over a million dollars for a safe delivery. Others are small boat owners who use their craft to land drug shipments at isolated spots along the American coast. Still other runners find ways to hide the drugs in big commercial airliners or in freighters bringing legal cargo from the drug-producing countries.

At the bottom of the drug pyramid are the street dealers—the ones who sell the drugs to the users. Some peddle the stuff directly. Others find they can make more money by offering quantities of drugs to addicts, who then push the drugs on street corners and in school yards. One young dealer boasts that he could take in a million dollars this way.

WHO ARE THE STREET DEALERS?

Drug dealers supply users with illegal drugs but may or may not themselves be drug abusers. It is common, though, for users to become dealers. What happens is simply this. The occasional, recreational use of drugs increases until it becomes a dependency. As the users crave more and more of the drug, some drift into dealing.

Selling drugs offers a few advantages to the drug abuser. Because it pays very well, it can provide money for drugs, with some left over for other expenses. The dealers can get their own drugs at "wholesale" prices. The user/dealers can also attract others to drugs, which makes them feel less like outcasts. And dealing gives some a feeling of accomplishment; they are, in effect, running a successful, although illegal business.

A young man, familiar with the teenage drug scene, wrote this about dealing:

> *Many kids sell dope at one time or another, not just poor kids either. It's an easy way for them to get extra money to party, for dates, and for extra drugs. Dealing can also make a kid feel important. This can serve as a reinforcement to keep on dealing.*[3]

The Cocaine Hotline in Summit, New Jersey, recently found a number of dealers among 165 women who admitted to cocaine abuse. The typical female cocaine user, the survey found, was white, twenty-nine years old, and earned about $500 a week. But because she spent about $450 a week on drugs, she had to raise even more money. Boyfriends or husbands were a frequent source of cash, along with stealing or dealing drugs.

A young man who, with his friend, was a drug dealer, says this about his trade:

> *You'd buy, let's say a pound [.5 kg] of pot. You break it up into sixteen bags. Usually we did it by eye, just broke it up, looked at them, made them even. We'd buy a pound [.5 kg] of pot for maybe $400. You'd have sixteen ounces [450 g]. You'd sell ten ounces [280 g] and the rest would be for your head, or you'd just keep an ounce or two [42 g] for your head and sell the other four or five ounces [127 g] for profit. If you were selling at $40 an ounce [28 g], that's $200 profit, and you get to keep the other ounce for yourself.*

A lot of times, I would try and sell it quick, sell it in quarter pounds [.1 kg] at a time. I'd sell the three ounces [85 g] for $110, below everybody else, and I'd break even and get an ounce [.28 g] for myself. But a lot of the times, I'd spend some of that money, so I'd end up going down even though I should have broken even.

A hundred hits of acid—that's usually where the profit was, 'cause you couldn't take too much of that at one time. You could sell that stuff quick. Three or four times, I made a good profit on that.

You'd buy a hundred hits of acid for $180 and sell them for $4 a hit. You could keep twenty of them and still make $140. I'd usually plan it around a rock concert. Let's say the concert was on Friday. I'd tell people about it on Tuesday. On Wednesday, I'd bring twenty hits and sell them right away. Then the word would get around to the certain people that I would want to be associated with. They'd come back and buy another fifty the next day. Then I'd have thirty hits left for Friday before the concert. Usually, I'd sell out and sometimes I'd even run back to get more.[4]

DEALERS IN TROUBLE

But dealing drugs is not without its risks. For one thing, dealers often have lots of money on them. This makes them good targets for robberies or muggings. Also, the drugs they sell are sometimes under weight, of poor quality, or have a harmful additive mixed in. Customers who realize that they've been sold "bum dope," as it is called, may try to punish or even kill the dealer.

Also, dealers do not always end up with a profit. Those who are drug abusers often use more of the drug than they sell. Many eventually find themselves in debt to the suppliers.

A drug dealer describes his problems:

It's dog-eat-dog as far as that's concerned. If you get ripped off, you can't go to the cops. If you got a big gang of friends . . . you might have a chance of getting your money back.

That's how I went, 'cause I didn't pay for it until I sold it. And 90 percent of the time I lost about 20 percent of the profit. I was twenty percent down from what the original cost of the dope was. I was always behind, so I was always making problems for myself and everybody else.[5]

In their book, *Doing Drugs*, Michael and Bruce Jackson add these comments:

Little wonder there is so much violence in the drug world. The thing about dealing is, everybody involved with it has the same motivation: greed. So you can't trust anyone, because everyone involved is concerned with making more and more money. It's a lot like gambling fever. It can become obsessive and compulsive, and it can get you into severe trouble. I know a sixteen-year-old who had to leave town in a hurry because the mob was after him for some money he got burned on in a coke deal.[6]

In that same book there are some observations on the dangers of drug dealing for young people:

Almost everyone who deals with the law is confident that he'll never get in trouble with the law. But what most kids fail to realize is that it is not just their risk. When a kid deals, he risks everything his parents have worked for. Lawyers' fees from a drug bust can reach $100,000. And that's not all the damage that is caused. The family gets hurt. There is a tremendous amount *of added stress when something like that happens. Public ridicule is also a drag. It leaves a long-lasting scar, not only on the kid who gets busted, but also on his parents and siblings whose public standings are also scarred.*[7]

HIDING THE DRUG MONEY

Just as drug users have the problem of raising money for drugs, so drug dealers have the problem of hiding the money they collect. Such activity is called "laundering." As you know, a laundry takes dirty clothes and makes them clean. Laundering money involves changing money that is "dirty" (from drug dealing) money and make it appear "clean" (from legitimate sources).

Odd as it may seem, the immense amount of currency that is collected by street dealers and suppliers is hard to handle. Think of someone on a busy street corner selling ten- and twenty-dollar vials of crack for several hours. No one pays with checks or credit cards. Everything is strictly cash. If business is good, the dealers' pockets bulge with five-, ten-, and twenty-dollar bills.

When the dealers' money reaches huge proportions, they fill large shopping bags and cardboard cartons with the cash. The simplest way to cut down the volume of small bills is to exchange them for currency of larger denomination—usually 100s—in cooperating banks. These banks feed the huge piles of small bills into high-speed money counters. When the volume is really heavy, they may just weigh the piles of money. It is known, for example, that 300 pounds (136 kg) of $20 bills is worth $3.6 million!

Exchanging small bills for large bills makes the drug money smaller in bulk. But what can be done with this money, which can run to millions of dollars a week? Investing these huge sums would be sure to attract attention. And spending it would surely invite the government to ask some very embarrassing questions.

So the top drug dealers and drug lords turn to money laundering. Here is how a typical scheme works: A drug dealer in Cleveland accumulates $10 million in cash. The dealer can't invest it or spend it. He can't even deposit the $10 million in a bank because by law the bank must report all transactions over $10,000 to the Internal Revenue Service.

The dealer looks for a bank where he can make a deal. Typically, he pays an officer of the bank a 2 percent fee ($200,000 on $10 million). In return, the banker accepts the deposit and "forgets" to file papers with the Internal Revenue Service.

The banker then wires the money to a bank outside the United States. Switzerland, Panama, Hong Kong, the Bahamas, and the Grand Cayman Islands in the Caribbean are the usual destinations. These countries allow banks to accept secret accounts, protecting the identity of the depositor. The money usually goes into the account of a false corporation controlled by the dealer.

The corporation then draws up papers showing that it is "loaning" the money to the dealer. It wires the money back to him. Now the dealer has the $10 million, less the various fees and bribes he paid for this complex transaction. Since the money is now clean, the dealer can spend it freely. And he doesn't even have to pay taxes on it, since it's not income but a loan!

The city of Miami, Florida, is the capital of the money-laundering industry. Along elegant Brickwell Avenue are offices of over a hundred banks from about twenty-five different countries. In addition, there are over forty branches of overseas and out-of-state banks and nearly fifty agencies representing foreign banks.

According to one estimate, there are more banks than supermarkets in Miami!

Agents of the U.S. Treasury Department believe that over one-third of all Miami banks share in the huge profits made in laundering illegal drug money. These banks are known to the authorities as "Coin-O-Washers." Around forty of them routinely fail to report cash deposits of over $10,000, as required by law. In fact, law enforcement officials think that at least four of the banks are actually controlled by drug traffickers.

One indication that gigantic amounts of drug money pass through the Miami banks is the huge annual cash surplus of the Florida banking system. The Florida banks routinely report cash surpluses of six to eight *billion* dollars a year. That is more than twice the usual surpluses of other state banking systems around the country. Experts guess that over half of the surplus is drug money.

Money-laundering schemes are difficult to uncover, and it is difficult to gather the evidence needed to prosecute those involved. Criminal violations, when found, can result in a maximum penalty of five years in prison and a $500,000 fine.[8]

The first Miami bank to be found guilty of money laundering by the Drug Enforcement Administration (DEA) was the Great American Bank. In 1982, the government accused the bank of operating a giant laundering operation that involved forty-one American and five foreign bank accounts. According to the DEA, the Great American Bank laundered $94 million in illegal drug profits over a period of fourteen months. The DEA claimed that the bank's failure to report the large currency transactions "wasn't due to the actions of an isolated employee but was, in fact, a bank practice."[9]

Most of the laundered money ends up in the pockets of the drug lords and supports their lavish life styles—expensive houses and apartments all over the world, fleets of private planes and yachts to meet their every desire, staffs of servants, the finest clothes, food, and entertainment that money can buy, and so on. But they also use some of their money to buy into legitimate businesses.

Thus, even if all drug dealing were to disappear tomorrow, the big drug lords would be left with controlling interests in many legal corporations, factories, stores, farms, and other commercial interests. Not only is the drug trade extracting a great deal of money from drug users and robbing the government of millions of dollars in tax revenues, it is also buying its way into the very heart of America's trade and industry.

8

DRUG
TRAFFICKING

The outdoor market in the tiny village of Zinahota in Bolivia is a bustling and colorful place. Peasants from the neighboring countryside join the three hundred residents of the town in buying and selling pigs, chickens, and basketfuls of onions, peppers, and brightly colored tropical fruits. Spread out on tables and on the ground are other things the merchants are selling—wonderful-smelling herbs and spices, shiny new pots and pans, and a strange assortment of shampoos and sweaters, bicycle tires and bottle openers, pictures and portable radios.

To the casual observer, Zinahota appears to be the same as any other country market. Yet it is different. Also for sale are big bags stuffed with small, bright-green leaves and smaller sacks filled with a brown powder. And it is these two products—the raw materials used in the manufacture of cocaine—that are the main items for sale in Zinahota. Together they are worth more than everything else in the market!

Illegal drugs are sold all over the world. But Zinahota is one of the few places where the drugs are sold out in the open. This is because the drug lords, who grow the coca plants and manufacture them into cocaine, are in complete control here. They will stop at nothing, even murder, to prevent officials from interfering with this activity.

What happens in Zinahota, and elsewhere in Bolivia, also occurs in Peru and Colombia in South America. And the same sort of trafficking goes on in the so-called "Golden Crescent"—Pakistan, Afghanistan, and Iran in the Middle East—and in the "Golden Triangle"—Burma, Laos, and Thailand in the Far East.

Does the drug trafficking in these distant lands impact on American society? Certainly! The activity in the producer nations rebounds on the economic, social, and political life of all other nations.

THE ECONOMIC EFFECTS

The first step in drug trafficking is to get the drugs from the various sources to the buyers, mostly in the United States and Europe. Traffickers transport the stuff in various ways. They hide the drugs inside hollowed-out logs, bales of fabrics, tin cans, or anything else that can possibly serve as a safe place. Then they place the goods aboard passenger ships, freighters, or airliners for the trip usually to America or Europe.

As the drugs make their way to the users, their price skyrockets. The heroin sold on the streets of America starts out as opium, a gummy material found in the seed pods of the poppy plant. A farmer in Pakistan who grows the poppy plants and extracts the opium gets around a thousand dollars for 10 kilograms (22 pounds).

From the grower, the opium goes to a processor who converts it into something called morphine base. The processor is paid about $1,200 for 10 kilos (22 pounds) of morphine base.

The morphine base goes next to the heroin manufacturer. In his laboratory, he changes the 10 kilos (22 pounds) of morphine base into one kilo (2 pounds) of heroin, which is worth about $15,000.

The distributor, who gets the pure heroin next, cuts or dilutes the drug many times over with such cheap substances as milk sugar, cornstarch, or even cleansing powder. He then packages the heroin, which is now only about 6 percent pure, in around 175,000 "dime bags." Each bag is a single dose of the drug and sells for $10. Thus the $1,000 worth of opium ends up with a street value of $1,750,000!

Cocaine, too, escalates in price as it passes from grower to distributor to dealer. The grower of coca plants in the Andes mountains of South America receives about $4,000 for 500 kilos (1,100 pounds) of the coca leaves from which cocaine is made. The 500 kilos (1,100 pounds) will produce only 8 kilos (18 pounds) of cocaine. But this cocaine sells on the street for at least $500,000!

Obviously, there are fantastic profits to be made in the drug trade. Mathea Falco, former Assistant Secretary of State for International Narcotics Matters, estimates that illicit drug sales in the United States alone run to about $80 billion per year! That's very, *very* big business. Only one legal American corporation, the oil giant Exxon, takes in more money annually.

Because of the huge sums that are involved, coca farming is extremely profitable. In Colombia, for example, the total drug trade adds about three billion dollars a year to the economy. For many peasants, the cultivation of coca plants serves as a way out of poverty. Instead of planting yucca, corn, and pineapples, farmers work in the coca trade. A worker tending traditional crops earns about five dollars a day. Caring for the coca crop can triple his income. Processing the coca into coca paste can make him wealthy. In Malaysia, a half million of the 15.7 million population are supported by the heroin trade.

The sudden acquisition of great wealth is immediately noticed in the less-developed countries. Take the Peruvian jungle town of Tingo Maria where the principal crop is coca.

The trade has brought immense sums of money into this tiny farming community within a short period of time. Along with this wealth came a demand for automobiles, trucks, and other luxury items. Used Chevettes, for example, were selling for $25,000. Small pickup trucks went for $35,000, Cadillacs and Lincolns were $100,000, and a Corvette or Mercedes fetched up to $350,000!

Many social scientists expect that cocaine use in the United States will decline by the 1990s. What will happen to those communities and nations who depend on cocaine trafficking?

Late in 1984, Colombia experienced just such a situation. With America's help, President Betancour launched an all-out war on drugs. He destroyed the coca crops and shut down many of the cocaine-processing labs. As a result, Colombia's national debt rose, the government was unable to attract foreign loans and investment, leftist rebels became more powerful, and dissent among peasants caused widespread chaos.

Drug-trafficking money also has an impact within the United States. In Miami and other resort communities where there is drug trafficking tourism suffers. The $10 billion annual industry of Miami, for example, has been particularly affected. Three years after *Time* magazine published an issue detailing Miami drug-related violence, one motel owner lost about 20 percent of his bookings. He said, "Some of my regular customers who have been staying here every winter since the 1960s have never come back. Now they go to the west coast of Florida where the drug scene is less visible."[1]

THE SOCIAL EFFECTS

The large profits that go to the drug traffickers are responsible for a rash of violent acts against people, property, and institutions. In Baton Rouge, Louisiana, a jury found three Colombians guilty of the murder of a key witness in a government drug case. The witness, Adler Seal, was a pilot who had earned more than $50 million smuggling cocaine and other drugs from South America to the United States.

Fifteen persons were arrested in California as the result of an organized crime investigation. Included were "capos," bosses of organized crime groups, as well as low-level "soldiers" and "associates" of the crime family. They were indicted for attempted murder as well as for trafficking in large amounts of cocaine.

Federal agents uncovered a scheme in which seventeen Colombian Airlines employees planned to transport illegally $10 million or more in U.S. currency to Colombia over a ten-month period. A month earlier, agents had broken up a ring—including employees of Pan Am, Delta, and Eastern airlines—that had smuggled almost $1.5 billion worth of cocaine into Kennedy International Airport in New York.

Enrique Bermudez, a low-level dealer, pleaded guilty in 1979 to selling a half-ounce (14 g) of cocaine to an undercover police officer. In return for a shorter sentence, Bermudez cooperated with the authorities. His testimony resulted in the imprisonment of several other dealers. Not long after Bermudez was released from a five-year prison term, while he was away at work, several traffickers entered his home and executed the two women and eight children who were present.

In 1982, Federal Judge John H. Wood, known as "Maximum John" for the stiff sentences he handed down, was killed to prevent him from presiding over a drug-trafficking case. The U.S. Embassy in Bogota was bombed and American diplomats and their families in Colombia were threatened with execution for interfering with the Colombian drug trade. DEA agent Enrique Salazar was kidnapped and murdered in Mexico. The killing was masterminded by drug traffickers, and carried out by corrupt Mexican police officers.

Organized crime groups, in particular the Mafia, smuggle in a large percentage of the drugs that enter the United States. Smuggling commands huge amounts of money—up to $32 billion annually for cocaine and more than $2 billion for heroin!

The authorities used to think that drugs entering this country came from separate sources. But they have since discovered that most of the drugs can be traced back to just a few gangsters connected with the Mafia. In April 1986, when federal agents picked up thirty-eight drug traffickers, they found that the leaders were all members of two well-known Mafia crime groups— the Lucchese and Genovese families.

There is every indication that the mob in America uses the same tactics of violence and bribery as their counterparts in Bolivia to establish their control. For example, there were about 150 gangland-style murders in the city of Miami in 1981 that the police said were drug related. During the period from 1980 to 1982, more than twenty-five Colombian drug dealers living in America were killed. Also, the FBI recently collected evidence that for more than twelve years a New York judge had been accepting bribes to fix cases for the mob, including some involving drug trafficking.

The rising tide of drugs smuggled into this country exposes more and more U.S. police officers to bribes

A trained German shepherd dog
searches a van for smuggled drugs

and payoffs. "It's not unusual for a patrol officer to stop a car in Miami on a routine traffic violation and find the guy has $20,000 or more in cash on him," said one high-ranking law enforcement official. "With some cops, sooner or later they're going to take the money one way or another. And that's just the beginning. It's hard to stop after that."[2]

In 1987, law enforcement authorities became aware that Chinese criminals in America, especially in New York, were taking over some of the drug trafficking formerly controlled by the Mafia. Officials of the DEA suggest some possible reasons: Police action and internal squabbling have weakened the Mafia; Chinese criminals have been getting bolder and more sophisticated; law enforcement has concentrated on the Mafia and ignored the Chinese crime groups.

"However you make your money," says writer T. D. Allman about Miami, "you know at least some of it has to be drug money, because in Miami drug money buys everything. It's on the table when you settle up your bridge scores; it's on the collection plate when you go to church."

Allman goes on to say, "In the Miami drug trade, you can earn more than on Wall Street. Even penny-ante traders can make $1.5 million annually."[3]

While Miami has a bigger problem than most American cities because of the high volume of cocaine smuggled in from Latin America, corruption is on the rise elsewhere as well. Recently, a federal grand jury indicted a Hardin County, Tennessee, sheriff on charges of protecting dealers and selling drugs.

Drugs pay for about one of every three recreational boats in Miami. "Maybe fifty percent carry some kind of contraband sometime," says Allman. Also, drug trafficking is responsible for piracy of recreational boats in waters off the coast of Florida. Some stolen vessels are used for transporting drugs. Others are seized because they are mistaken for rival drug craft.

Dealers in security equipment, including pistols and rifles, tout their wares at national boat shows in Florida. As one Miami gun-shop owner put it:

Although the homeowner is the major buyer of guns here, yachtmen and fishermen probably rank second. So many of them cruise these lonely waters . . . that there's no way they're going without at least a .38 or .45 handgun. Corrosion-proof firearms are the most popular.[4]

And this is what a Miami firearms instructor stated:

By and large, when they're [boat owners] out on the high seas in the no-man's land of the cocaine cowboys, they want something that will let bullets fly. In fact, they want training with the same things that the drug runners carry—automatics and semiautomatics like the UZI and MAC-10.[5]

Sometimes, boating people get caught up in the drug-trafficking trade themselves. On August 29, 1987, powerboat champion Benjamin Kramer was arrested for running a drug ring involving the distribution of more than 550,000 pounds [250,000 kg] of marijuana between March 1980 and June 1987. The grand jury said Mr. Kramer was the "organizer, supervisor and manager" of the smuggling ring, which operated in Florida, Illinois, and elsewhere in the United States.[6]

POLITICAL EFFECTS

Perhaps the biggest political problem caused by drugs is the wholesale corruption of individuals and institutions. In some trafficking areas, government corruption is so widespread that it is considered normal. In southern Florida, drug-related corruption in law enforcement has become so common that reports of new scandals usually do not even appear in the newspapers.

Perhaps the most frightening political aspect of drug trafficking is that the drug-dominated, unofficial government functions alongside the officially elected one. It is a government within the government; its leaders are not bound by the laws that rule everyone else.

Either by violence, the threat of violence, or bribery, the drug traders and traffickers have taken control in many areas around the world. Frightened or corrupt officials exist at every level of government—from national leaders to small-town policemen. Taxes are not collected, laws are broken, criminals are not punished, and a general lawlessness and lack of respect for the institutions of society becomes prevalent. In this way, the traffickers take over political control of anything from an individual city or neighborhood to a whole country.

Bolivian Attorney General Carlos Mauro Hoyos summed up the role of traffickers in politics: "Narcotics traffickers are becoming a superstate because of their enormous wealth. But if we allow ourselves to be intimidated by fear or by the power of these people, our future will be more and more uncertain."[7]

Bolivia, perhaps more than any other country, has been affected by the politics of drugs, and the officials there are not optimistic for the future. The violence of the drug traffickers and the immense wealth they have accumulated have virtually paralyzed the government. Members of the Bolivian Congress received the money for their election campaigns from the leaders of the drug rings and are reluctant to turn on these supporters. Both major political parties—the Liberals and Conservatives—have ties to the major drug traders. The police and armed forces don't act, either from fear or because they have taken bribes.

The court system is of little help. By early 1987, a

total of fifty-seven judges plus the justice minister had been murdered, either for sentencing a drug trader or for refusing a payoff. The surviving judges are now afraid to rule against the drug dealers. Even the anti-government communist terrorists have accepted funding from drug money.

The church and the press are also involved. Until 1984, the Catholic Church was able to justify accepting donations from the drug bosses. While newspaper reporters have been one of the few groups that has fought the cocaine crime gangs, they have paid a price. From 1984 to 1987, a total of twenty-four reporters have been killed.

Drug traffickers are bold enough to attempt government take-overs quite openly. In 1980, for example, the outcome of the presidential race in Bolivia was undecided. Before that nation's congress could meet to decide the issue, army commander General Luis Garcia Meza, a major cocaine trafficker, staged a military coup. He then proceeded to set up close links between the government and the nation's drug enterprises.

Sometimes the drug traffickers work with international terrorist groups. Activities of the Palestine Liberation Organization, the Syrians in the Bakaa Valley, the communist insurgents in Burma, the M-19 leftist rebels in Colombia, and the Shining Path guerrillas in Peru are financed and armed by the illegal drug industry.

Some say that U.S. efforts to destroy drugs at the source by military means is a new source of weapons supply for third-world countries. Several countries, including Bolivia, Colombia, Thailand, Pakistan, and Burma are using weapons provided for the antidrug war to kill anyone who disagrees with their politics.

U.S. government officials suspect that the leader of Panama, General Manuel Antonio Noriega, accepts payoffs of millions of dollars a year to allow drug shipments to pass through Panama on their way to the United States. The payments are protection money for the drug traffickers, who are permitted to go about their business without police interference.

Drug experts disagree about how to reduce drug abuse. Some say cut the trafficking and demand will dry up. Others say that trafficking will end when demand is curbed. But they all agree that drug trafficking, with its close connection to organized crime, is a disease that is hurting our nation. It is a disease that needs to be treated and cured!

9
TOLL ON
THE FAMILY

Three words describe Kathy—pretty, bright, and bubbly. But somehow she was always in trouble. When she was in junior high school, she ran away from home twice. During high school, she was picked up by the police for shoplifting four times. By graduation time, she had developed a $75-a-day cocaine habit.

Kathy's parents tried over and over again to get her to give up the drugs and other bad behavior. Each time they spoke to her, Kathy said the same thing, "I'm sorry. This time I'm really going to stop."

Since her family adored Kathy, they believed her. They accepted her excuses and forgave her. They thought that showing Kathy how much they loved her would make her change her ways. After all, they told each other, we care so much for her that she would not want to hurt us. Yet, Kathy always returned to drugs and to stealing to pay for her habit.

As a matter of fact, Kathy didn't want to hurt her folks or her two brothers and sister. Nevertheless, she continued doing drugs. She felt that she could not stop.

Eventually, Kathy moved in with a dealer who promised her all the coke she wanted. One night, though, he got angry and beat her severely. Kathy suffered a black eye, some broken teeth, and a badly cut lip.

When Kathy came running home, her family was horrified to see her condition. But they were very glad to have her back. Perhaps now she would listen to them.

Yet, after only a few weeks, Kathy returned to her dealer-boyfriend. This made her parents very angry and frustrated. Also, they were embarrassed at what the neighbors would think, hurt that she did such a thing to them, fearful that Kathy was already an addict, and guilty for having failed as parents.

They blamed the school. "It's the school's fault. They don't do enough to combat drugs."

They blamed television. "It's because of television. Kids learn about drugs from television."

They blamed the dealers. "The cops should do a better job of getting rid of them."

They blamed the neighborhood. "The kids around here are bad. Had we moved years ago this would not have happened."

But most of all they blamed each other for Kathy's problems.

"You were too soft."

"You were too strict."

"You spoiled her."

"You didn't show her enough love."

"You smothered her."

"You didn't spend enough time with her."

Widespread drug use in America created what was called "a major social problem" in the late 1960s and early 1970s. In the rush to handle this crisis the focus was almost exclusively on the individual drug user. Now, however, the focus is turning more to the drug user as a member of a family group and as a member of society. Perhaps Dr. Edgar H. Auerswald, Director of the Maui Community Health Center, Wailuku, Hawaii, summed it up best when he wrote: "I have come to the conclusion that, if our country is serious in its apparent wish to attack the phenomenon of drug abuse, the way to do so is *not* to develop drug abuse programs, but instead to develop a system that will support and foster family life."[1]

PARENTS AND SIBLINGS

Kids give many different reasons for saying yes to drugs. Among them are peer pressure, rebellion against parents and authority, feelings of rejection, low self-esteem, hopelessness, excess pressure to perform, curiosity and experimentation, relief from depression, pain, stress, desire to overcome inhibitions and shyness, boredom, lack of goals and aimlessness, maintaining an image, and a need to hide their inadequacies.

Richard E. Blum, of Stanford University, gives still another reason. "People learn to use drugs from the same respected older people who teach them other things about living—primarily their parents."[2] This is a reason given despite the fact that almost all parents object to drug abuse. According to one study, over 97 percent of high school seniors said that their parents would disapprove of their smoking marijuana regularly, of taking LSD or amphetamines, or of having four or five drinks a day.[3]

However, kids learn more from what parents do than what they say. They watch—and copy—the way their parents may fight depression and deal with stress. Attitudes make drug use permissible. Behavior can give out the message that at the first hint of pain or discomfort, fear or anxiety, the child should take some "feel-good" pills or medicine.

Also, kids learn to take drugs by identifying and modeling themselves after older brothers and sisters who use drugs. Siblings of teenage drug abusers are at a higher risk than those who do not have an older family member who has a drug habit.

Once a youngster begins doing drugs, he or she may be rejected by the other members of the family. The abuser often makes the situation worse by pulling away from the others. Within a very short period of time, the teenaged abuser may have separated from parents and siblings emotionally, if not in a physical sense.

The siblings frequently react with danger, hostility, and frustration to the drug user. Sometimes they blame the user for getting into drugs—and take out their annoyance on them. Fights and arguments follow, and the family evolves a pattern of ongoing conflict and hostility.

A teenager recently described his parents' reactions to his drug-taking this way:

> At the beginning, I think they hated me. They've never once told me that they hated me or they didn't want me or they wanted me to leave or anything like that. They've always said, "I love you, you're my child." But they reacted really bad. My father is a very violent man, and when he found out that stuff he didn't say one word and he didn't do much about it, and that's what killed me more than anything. I wish he would have hit me or something and got it all out, but he didn't do anything. That's what hurt me the most.[4]

Of course, siblings sometimes identify with drug users. The other children view them as being able to get away with things. So, the others try the same behavior. Or they may be afraid of the drug users and try to imitate them. This is known as "identification with the aggressor." It is like kids mimicking the bully on the block in the hope that he will not harass them if they are like him.

In some cases, the family unconsciously works to

keep the abuser on drugs. The continuing drug abuse becomes a way of maintaining a relationship between parents who might otherwise drift apart. Or it is a way of prolonging childhood and keeping the adolescent in a dependent state. Although the parents may express anger at the child's illegal activities, they may also shower him or her with extra attention and even provide money for drugs. One mother repeatedly supplied her adult children with heroin because she "did not want to see them suffer." As the researcher of this case concluded, sometimes "drug taking helps to maintain family stability."[5]

Making believe the problem doesn't exist, getting angry and blaming everyone, and identifying with the user are a few ways families try to adjust to the drug problem of one member. None of these methods is particularly healthy. They all create other difficulties.

OTHER LOVED ONES

People are known to neglect jobs, family, and their own personal welfare to get a steady supply of drugs. The shock waves that this sends out can damage or destroy personal as well as professional relationships.

Take George, a twenty-seven-year-old manager at a large shoe store, who was hooked on cocaine. "All I could think about was coke. I wanted more of it more often. Everything else seemed unimportant."

George lost his job after he was arrested for breaking into a house and stealing silverware and money. He confessed that he had been breaking into homes for over a year to get money to pay for the drugs he craved.

His personal and family life was also a mess. He couldn't find another job in the small town where he lived. He had no money to pay the rent and buy the food for his family. And his wife was threatening to leave and take their two-year-old daughter with her.

Yet, George denies that drugs are the problem. This denial is due to the way the drugs have changed his thinking. He finds it hard to recognize the difference between right and wrong. And he refuses to enter treatment to break his drug habit and straighten out his life.

It is not unusual for cocaine or some other drug to take the place of loving and caring feelings between people. The user's feelings are built on the false emotions of the drugs. On drugs, he feels good; off them, he feels bad. Because good feelings fade quickly, disappointment and dissatisfaction often follow.

A study of 307 addicts points out the impact of heroin abuse on family life. The researchers found that daily users were arrested an average of 2.18 times a year for drug offenses and 1.79 times a year for other crimes. The nondaily users had only 0.99 arrests per year for their drug use and 0.75 arrests a year for crimes not connected with drugs. The same study also collected information on the employment situation of heroin addicts. The authors found that daily heroin users held jobs only 39 percent of the time. This compared unfavorably with the nondaily users who were working 63.5 percent of the time.[6]

The poor employment statistics of the strongly addicted also tell something about the conditions within the family. Where there is no regular source of income, a whole range of problems follows. With an average of four arrests a year and working less than half the time, there are just three possible solutions for the addicts: They can deal drugs. They can steal. Or they can go on welfare. None offers any real hope for developing a stable family structure.

WOMEN AND CHILDREN

The rise of cocaine use, especially crack, has been particularly damaging to women and children. As crack has replaced heroin as the favorite hard drug among the young of the inner city, a far higher proportion of women have become addicts.

Hale House, a rehabilitation home for drug-addicted babies in New York City, is finding that incoming babies now tend to suffer from crack, not heroin, addiction. According to Mother Clara Hale, the eighty-two-year-old founder of Hale House, the one thing the infants have in common is a mother who used crack.

Because many poor families are now headed by single mothers, the sudden jump in women crack addicts has caused a disproportionate damage to families. It has also produced a rise in child abuse, neglect, and death connected to drug use by parents. Crack addiction has become associated far more often with erratic and violent behavior than heroin, for example.

The problem is seen in the growing number of "boarder babies"—infants, neglected or abandoned by their parents, who remain in hospitals because their parents have given them up and foster parents will not take them in. For weeks and sometimes months, hundreds of generally healthy babies born to crack addicts languish in hospital cribs. These babies, who are seldom held or nurtured, are just waiting for someone to find them homes.

Father John Fagan of Brooklyn agrees. At any given time, he takes care of a small number—about ten—of these boarder babies from New York City through his "Little Guys Program." In 1987 he placed over three hundred of them in either temporary or permanent homes.

Many fear the worst impact of the boarder baby situation is yet to come. As Dr. Bernard Bihari, director of the addiction unit at Kings County Hospital in Brooklyn, New York said, "We may not see for years the full effect on the children."[7]

Of course, drug abuse has had a serious effect on poor women and their children since the 1960s. But the

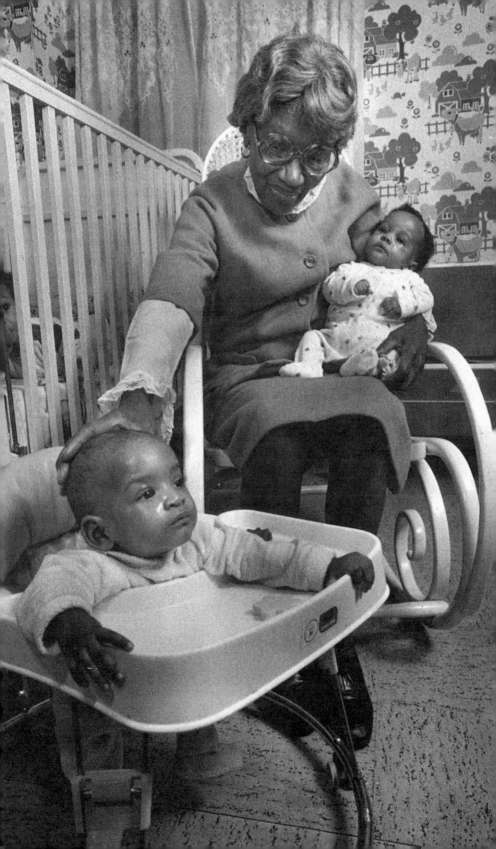

shift from heroin to cocaine seems to be making the impact more devastating. The destruction of the family among black people is especially grave, according to Beny J. Primm, executive director of a drug-treatment program that serves a high proportion of black mothers who are addicts. He says, "It [crack] is such a devastating addiction that these people are willing to abandon food and water and child to take care of their crack habit."[8]

Eric Brettschneider, of the New York City Human Resources Administration, points out that the number of cases of neglected or abused children rose 30 percent from June 1985 to June 1986—an increase also attributed to the use of crack by parents. "We see cases where children are left alone without supervision when parents go out to get drugs," he said. "Or a parent becomes overwhelmed with drug needs and loses sight of feeding the child."[9]

Clinical observations show that such newborns are less alert and less attentive. There is little or no mother-infant interaction. This may lead to impaired development in the first year of life.

The children born to drug abusers suffer a wide variety of health defects. Infants born to mothers taking heroin or barbiturates are found to be hyperactive, restless, and to suffer from tremors, to have difficulty in sleeping, and not to be able to concentrate.

If the mother is on marijuana, her baby tends to have a lower birth weight. Babies of mothers who have abused cocaine, marijuana, or PCP are born with a

Mother Clara Hale at Hale House —the Harlem home for infants born drug-addicted. She has devoted her life to helping little ones such as these.

number of severe birth defects. But most of the problems are much less significant after one year.

Mothers on methadone tend to have babies with eye and ear disorders, poor motor skills, and slow speech and language development.

Dr. Leonard Glass, of Kings County Hospital in Brooklyn, New York, found that between one-third and one-half of all the babies born to crack-using mothers had neurological problems. These included irritability, tremors, and muscle stiffness. In general, Dr. Glass says, these conditions begin to disappear by about the fourth day. He compared that with the condition of children of heroin addicts, who have similar symptoms, but which last for up to two weeks.

Of course, it may be that the lower birth weight of some infants results, not from the mother's drug habit, but rather her poor nutrition. Also, some of the slowness of development may be due to parents who can't, won't, or don't know how to provide a stimulating environment for their child's growth. In all these areas, further research is needed.

10

DRUGS IN THE WORKPLACE

"Hi," the voice said on the call to 800-COCAINE, the cocaine hotline. "I'm an airline pilot. But I don't want to give you my name or the airline I work for."

"That's okay," the person answering the phone replied. "What can we do for you?"

"I'm heavily into coke," the pilot continued. "I've been snorting steady for three days straight—no sleep, no food, no nothing, just sniffing the stuff. Right now I'm real beat and my head is not on straight."

"Yes, go on," the counselor said encouragingly.

"Tonight I'm supposed to take a 747 to Paris. I think I could do it. But I'm scared. And if something should go wrong . . ." the pilot's voice trailed off.

A pause. Then, in a weak voice, the pilot asked, "What do you think I should do?"

"It's simple," the counselor immediately replied. "Call in sick and go to sleep. Then tomorrow give us another call and we'll see about getting you some help."

This call to the cocaine hotline from someone worried about drugs and work is not unusual. In a recent study conducted by the 800-COCAINE counselors, 75 percent of those calling the hotline reported that they sometimes took coke while on the job. About 69 percent said they regularly worked under the influence of cocaine, and 25 percent said they used cocaine at work every day.

No one knows the full extent of drug use on the job in the United States. But there is no doubt that during the past twenty years illegal drugs have become a significant problem in the nation's workplaces. Almost everywhere—offices and factories, stores and farms, restaurants and warehouses—workers are getting high on marijuana, cocaine, and other illegal drugs.

The concern that drugs interfere with work is so great that about one third of the Fortune 500 companies, the largest private corporations in America, have started drug-testing programs. As Robert W. Waggart of Southern Pacific Railroad said, "When you come to work with drops of marijuana used on the weekend in your system, statistically I know that you will cost me more in productivity, in health-care costs, and in absenteeism."[1] Peter Bensinger, former chief of the DEA, holds a similar view. "If somebody smokes pot on Saturday night, it's the employer's business on Monday."[2]

Research indicates that people who take drugs regularly—some 25 percent of the population according to government calculations—are likely to use them at work or at least sometimes be stoned or on a high when they arrive at the workplace. Federal experts estimate that up to 23 percent of all U.S. workers use dangerous drugs on the job; as many as 7 percent actually use the drugs while at work every day. A survey conducted for the NIDA indicates that nearly two-thirds of those between the ages of eighteen and twenty-five have used illicit drugs. And even more, 44 percent, have used them in the past year.[3]

Employee abuse of drugs creates all sorts of problems for American businesses. The major concerns are accidents, theft, loss of productivity, absenteeism, and added health costs.

ACCIDENTS

Drug abusers cause more on-the-job accidents than nondrug users. The fatigue caused by spending whole nights doing drugs, the distortion of perception and hallucinations, the reduced ability to think clearly and use good judgment, and the lower level of manual skills all contribute to injuries and mishaps. One estimate says that drug abusers are responsible for between three and four times the number of accidents caused by nondrug users.

The greatest worry, of course, is in those jobs where mistakes can cost lives. Between 1975 and 1985 about fifty train accidents were attributed to drug- or alcohol-impaired workers. In those accidents, thirty-seven people were killed, eighty were injured, and more than $34 million worth of property was destroyed.

Drug use was implicated in the January 4, 1987, collision of an Amtrack passenger train and three Conrail freight locomotives near Baltimore. Sixteen people were killed and 175 others were injured in this, the worst accident in Amtrack history. Amtrack chairman, W. Graham Claytor, said he was convinced that the Conrail engineer and brakeman "must have been impaired" by drug use because tests showed marijuana in their blood and urine.[4]

In a 1983 air accident, two men died when their private plane crash-landed at Newark airport. An autopsy showed the presence of marijuana in the pilot's blood, a sign that he might have been smoking marijuana while flying. Two years later, an air-traffic controller with a 3-gram-(.1-ounce)-a-day cocaine habit nearly caused a collision between a private plane and a jumbo jet.

A Chicago-based electric utility started an antidrug program in 1982, offering treatment to any users who came forward. Since the program started, absenteeism is down 25 percent and medical claims, which had been rising at an average of 23 percent annually, went up only 6 percent. Moreover, the company had fewer on-the-job accidents in 1985 than in any previous year. "I don't think that all of the improvements are directly related to the drug program," says Vice President J. Patrick Sanders. "But it's got to be more than coincidental."[5]

Many consider the incidence of drug abuse in the armed forces an especially alarming problem. An accident while flying a fighter plane, operating a nuclear submarine, or even firing a gun, can be responsible for the loss of many lives.

Drug abuse became a big problem during the Vietnam War. Military people were performing many tasks requiring great care and accuracy. Some experts claimed that high levels of drug use cost the nation considerable numbers of injuries and lost lives.

In December 1976, a study of the sailors on the aircraft carrier U.S.S. *Midway* showed that a full 20 percent of the sailor population were using narcotics and other drugs. At about the same time, the heroin overdose death rate of U.S. Army soldiers in Europe was three times as high as the civilian heroin overdose death rate. A survey conducted by the Navy found that 33 percent of all seamen admitted to using illegal drugs—mostly marijuana—within the previous month.

Some members of Congress were very distressed by the findings. Hearings were held to determine if the security of the United States was being threatened by the high level of drug abuse in the military. In 1980, after concluding that drugs were indeed a problem in the armed forces, the Department of Defense began a study to learn the extent of drug abuse among military personnel. A total of 15,268 randomly selected men and women, stationed at eighty-one military bases, were questioned.

Marijuana showed up as the most abused drug among the enlisted members of the armed services. Of those using drugs, 21 percent reported some negative effect on their work performance from their use. The results led the Department of Defense to try to curb the use of illicit drugs in the military through a program of drug testing and counseling. Testing for marijuana became the main goal of the Defense Department. Members of the service did not have the right to refuse testing, but they could contest the results.

The Air Force has recently begun requiring drug tests for all crew members and ground personnel involved in airplane disasters. It is up to the commander to decide whether or not to test in less serious accidents.

From 1981 to 1986, the armed forces cut the use of illicit drugs by two-thirds. In the process, they discharged 64,485 people. The use of marijuana has been cut to one-third that among civilians of comparable age, according to statistics from the Pentagon and the NIDA.[6]

THEFT

The presence of drugs on the job is undermining the honesty and reliability of the American labor force. Addicts with costly habits are much more likely than others to steal cash from a company safe, products from a warehouse, or tools from a factory.

Employers are concerned that drug abusers cannot be trusted to handle expensive items or keep business and trade secrets within the firm. Another danger is that the worker's mind is so clouded by the drug that he or she makes serious mistakes in counting money, or misplaces valuable jewels, or something similar. There is also the possibility that drug-abusing workers will give confidential information to competitors in return either for drugs or for the money to buy drugs.

Drug abuse makes the headlines when it involves Hollywood celebrities and sports stars. But the problem is also widespread among employees in many high-pressure, fast-paced work environments.

- A jury in New Jersey found Police Officer Anthony Ruffin, an eighteen-year veteran of the force, guilty of selling cocaine while in uniform.
- A former employee at a computer company tells of selling cocaine for three years to the people who worked with him.
- A stockbroker who was recovering from his addiction described snorting cocaine in his office, in mens' rooms, even in elevators. "It woke me up and gave me strength," he says. "It made me feel like J. P. Morgan."
- A New Jersey dentist injected himself with three syringes of cocaine every morning before work until he began to complain that the fillings he was putting into patients' mouths were talking to him.
- Dr. Howard Frankel, medical director of Rockwell's space shuttle division from 1981 to 1983, says that he treated employees who were hallucinating, collapsing from cocaine overdoses, and using marijuana, PCP, heroin, and numerous other drugs while at work. According to his estimates, 20 to 25 percent of the Rockwell workers at the Palmdale, California, plant, the final assembly point for the space shuttles, were high on the job from drugs, alcohol, or both. During the construction of the spacecraft, undercover agents were able to buy cocaine, heroin, amphetamines, and marijuana from employees. This led to a raid by police on Rockwell's shuttle assembly plant. As a result, nine workers were fired.

Obviously, any drug abuse among production workers in the space program or the defense industry carries grave risks. Says Dr. Frankel, "In this kind of ultra-high-tech work, the guy who makes the little adjustments, the screwer-on of parts, the bolter of nuts, is just as important as the project's chief engineer."[7]

Besides fearing that stoned employees may do shoddy work on missiles and planes, defense-industry executives are concerned about protecting information from theft or disclosure. Addicts on the payroll might sell defense secrets to support their habits. Narcotics-possession charges have led to the loss of the security clearances necessary for many jobs in the defense industry, making the drug abusers extremely vulnerable to blackmail. Says R. Richard Heppe, the president of Lockheed California: "We do a lot of highly classified work here, and people with these problems are much higher security risks."[8]

Because some drug abuse encourages stealing, companies that specialize in investigating employee theft have been sprouting up everywhere. One such firm, called Loss Management, found that a particular company's invoices did not add up correctly. A careful check showed that three top managers at the company were embezzling money to buy cocaine!

DROP IN PRODUCTIVITY

Drug abuse costs the nation about $100 billion every year in lost production. Carlton E. Turner, director for the White House Drug Abuse Police Office, says that private-sector employers know that the drug user has only about two-thirds' the output of other employees.

Some drugs are consumed in long, late-night, or all-night sessions. In these cases, just the lack of sleep makes the workers inefficient the following day. One worker said marijuana makes him feel lazy. He said, "I get a cloudy feeling in my head."

Not long ago a research team studied the effect on pilots' skills after smoking a single marijuana cigarette. The pilots were first tested before taking the drug. All did extremely well. But when tested one and four hours after smoking marijuana, none of the ten pilots in the study could handle a plane nearly as well. Almost all said they felt "high." Most were barely able to control the plane. Twenty-four hours later the pilots were tested once again and still showed some degree of impairment.

Some workers actually do drugs while on the job. Cocaine users, for example, take the drug at work because they believe the drug helps them do their jobs better and faster. They have devised clever ways of taking the drug. One trick is to fill an empty squeeze-bottle with cocaine and keep it in a pocket, ready for sniffing. There are reportedly some dealers who deliver cocaine and marijuana directly to their customers' desks. And users sometimes send messengers on false errands to pick up packages that actually contain narcotics.

It's not only low-level employees who indulge in drugs while on the job. Managers, too, take time from work to do drugs on the sly. "Companies never think of drug use on the executive level," says Special Agent George Miller of the DEA. "They always think it's on the assembly line."

Naomi Behrman, a counselor for AT&T/Bell Labs, has the same opinion: "You can no longer assume that because a person wears a three-piece suit and a necktie, you can rule out drug abuse." For example, a $19-million legal action charged an attorney with spending

*A drug-abusing businessman
snorting cocaine in his office*

$2 million of his client's money on cocaine. And, in another case, the chairman of a liquor company was arrested after being discovered with $8,000 worth of cocaine.

Not only are drug users less productive than non-drug users, but they are often more irritable and harder to get along with. Drug-impaired workers are not always able or willing to shoulder their share of the work load. This often leads to stress, fights, and generally bad relations among the workers.

The mental problems associated with drug use also interfere with a person's working life. Concern with marital, financial, and legal problems outside of work frequently spills over and hurts job productivity.

Since drug-abusing workers make more mistakes and have more accidents on the job, the products they are turning out are of lower quality. Some even say that you should never buy an automobile that was manufactured on a Monday because many workers on the assembly line are not functioning very well after a weekend of partying!

ABSENTEEISM AND HIGHER COSTS

Drug abuse by workers can

- vastly increase health care costs and worker absenteeism.
- lead to ten or more times the normal absenteeism.
- cost the company three times as much in health-insurance fees.[9]

Companies lose money because of their drug-abusing employees. As was mentioned, the cost of drug abuse at work is estimated at around $100 billion. Who pays for all this? Every one of us. Companies have to charge more to make up for their drug-caused losses. If we want the product or the service they are selling, we have to pay the price.

In some places, drugs have begun to be used as currency. A number of advertising agencies, for example, use cocaine almost like money. A supply of cocaine for the models, photographers, and artists is provided as part of the basic budget. A recent survey of three hundred advertising directors reported forty-five cases in which cocaine had been used as under-the-counter payment. Some ad agency employees, it is said, make commercials only if the firms offer them bribes of cocaine.

At the same time, drug abuse on the job can wreck careers and lead to personal bankruptcy and even homelessness. One Wall Street trader was so hooked on cocaine that he lost his job and wound up living on the street and eating out of garbage cans. An attorney, who consumed about sixty thousand dollars a year of cocaine, thought that invisible people were watching him at all hours. His mental condition finally deteriorated to the point that he needed to be hospitalized.

But perhaps the most blatant example of the dangers of mixing drugs and work was reported by Dr. Robert Wick, corporate medical director of American Airlines. A computer operator, who was high after smoking a joint of marijuana, failed to load a crucial tape into a major airline's computer reservations system. The result? The system broke down for about eight hours, costing the company about $19 million. Says Wick: "That was an awfully expensive joint by anybody's standard."

11

DRUGS AND ROLE MODELS

Len Bias was a 6-foot, 8-inch (200-cm) -tall All-American star forward at the University of Maryland. The young basketball player was considered a model of clean living. On June 18, 1986, Bias signed a professional contract with his favorite team, the Boston Celtics, making a dream of his come true. But early in the morning of June 19, the superb athlete died suddenly in his dormitory room at the university.

Headlines all over the country announced the tragic news that Len Bias had been the victim of cocaine overdose. Before the end of the month, another young sports star, Don Rogers, died of a similar drug overdose. These sad occurrences alerted people, as never before, to the widespread abuse of drugs among star athletes and the dangers it poses—especially to the young.

Most religious and civic leaders agree that the character of a nation is shaped by its outstanding citizens—men and women in the worlds of sports, entertainment, business, and politics. Such personalities are the role models for the country's youth. They set the moral tone for all of society. Their behavior is widely followed and imitated by people in every walk of life.

When prominent athletes do drugs, it sends out a message that says, "Drugs are okay; they're cool. They don't interfere with performance or ability." The involvement of popular sports stars with drugs practically invites fans and followers to do the same.

Then there is another aspect. Famous athletes sometimes report that they wanted to break their drug habit, but just could not do it. The knowledge that these bigger-than-life characters couldn't stop makes young people experimenting with drugs begin to wonder, "What chance do I have?"

From time to time a state governor, a representative in Congress, or a federal official is found to be heavily dependent on drugs. Even though few of them deal or steal to get the money for drugs, they are still breaking the law each time they get high. When individuals pledged to uphold the laws of the land become lawbreakers, ordinary citizens become disillusioned. Some begin to think that what's all right for government officials is all right for them as well.

Famous singers, dancers, actors, and musicians make headlines when heavy drug use ruins their careers. Youngsters who are working very hard to develop their own performing skills become disillusioned. On some level, they start to distrust their ambition and question their artistic goals. They may even begin to doubt that artistic accomplishment brings the happiness and satisfaction they're seeking.

The press follows every action of the nation's public figures. Each incident involving drug abuse becomes a matter of public knowledge. This notoriety affects our behavior and attitude about drugs.

SPORTS

Drug abuse in sports came to the attention of the public in 1984 and 1985. It grew around a sensational criminal drug trial of players for the Pittsburgh Pirates. As a result, Peter Ueberroth, commissioner of baseball, proposed mandatory periodic random drug testing for major-league players.

The baseball commissioner believes, like many of our nation's leaders, that major-league players are role models to the youth of the nation. In addition, Ueberroth said, "Baseball wants to be a leader in setting an example—solving our drug problems."

Drugs, especially alcohol, have been part of sports in America for a long time. But the players' involvement with illegal drugs is somewhat more recent. In a television interview, former pitching star Dock Ellis described how he had taken drugs over the course of the twelve years that he played in the major leagues. Before one no-hit game, he confessed, he had taken LSD and was "tripping" the entire time. Apparently no one knew or seemed to care.

More recently, Lawrence Taylor, one of the legendary superstars of football, in his 1987 autobiography, *LT: Living on the Edge* (written with David Falker), told of using drugs, particularly cocaine and its more powerful derivative, crack, during the 1985 football season.

Taylor says he is not sure when he first started using cocaine. In the early days, though, he could control his desire for the drug. "I could do it and I could stop it," he insisted. "I knew what I was doing . . . how much to use."

But as time went on, he writes, "I started giving myself excuses to use cocaine." And the amount he took continued to increase. "Where I had been using half of a gram [.01 ounce] over a month," he said, "I was using a good part of that in a single evening. Twice a month became three times a week and maybe more."

By the middle of the 1985 season, Taylor realized that drugs were hurting his skill and ability as a ballplayer. "I knew that I was no longer going at 100 percent. But I also knew that my 75 percent was better than most other guys' 100 percent."

*Ricky Henderson of the New York Yankees (left)
and St. Louis Cardinals' Vince Coleman (center)
participate in a drug awareness program called
"Pros for Kids" run by Delvin Williams, executive
director, (right). During the 1987 season, for each
base stolen by Henderson and Coleman, the Mizuno
Corporation sponsored a free baseball session for
a youngster at a camp run by "Pros for Kids."*

During the entire period of his drug use, as Taylor said, "I made no effort to hide it." But he did keep a small bottle filled with urine from a drug-free player at hand. Then, when someone asked Taylor for a urine sample for a drug test, he substituted the one that he knew would test negative.

Taylor was open about his drug habit because he believed that no one, not his team, the National Football League, the police, or the press would do anything to stop his career. He was confident that he would not be punished, "as long as I was who I was and my game was intact."

"If I were Joe Blow," Taylor went on to say, "there'd be the slammer or some midnight trip to Betty Ford's farm [for drug rehabilitation]. . . . It was almost a thrill in itself knowing that people knew what I was doing and wouldn't do a damn thing to stop me."

But late in 1985, Taylor changed his attitude about drugs. "Drugs were a way of escaping rather than dealing with my problems. . . . [They] took me away from the people I love and care about most." Soon afterward Taylor entered a drug-rehabilitation program in Houston, Texas. The treatment was successful and Taylor broke his drug habit.[1]

More recently, Dwight Gooden, one of the youngest and most successful pitchers in the major leagues returned to the game after a program of drug therapy at a hospital in New York City. The story of his meteoric career rise, his brief fall from grace owing to drugs, and his outstanding return to peak form was followed closely in the media and the ballpark.

The public's first glimpse of trouble came during the 1986 season when Gooden started slipping in performance as compared to previous seasons. Rumors started to circulate: "Gooden was just a flash in the pan." "He just doesn't care anymore." "He's too young and can't take the pressure."

Then, during spring training in 1987, Gooden failed a routine urine test. The Mets' management suggested the pitcher go for drug treatment. Under the full gaze of media lights and attention, Gooden entered the Smithers Drug Rehabilitation program in New York. After a few weeks of treatment, Gooden was released. The ball club assigned him to pitch a few games with a minor-league farm club in Tidewater, Virginia. Before long he was allowed to return to the Mets and to his place on the mound. The fans' tremendous outpouring of love and affection was sustained during an outstanding pitching season.

As Gooden continues to wage a successful battle against drug dependence, many wonder: Did drugs become a problem for Gooden because he was a rich and famous superstar athlete? Does he have a greater responsibility to lead an exemplary life than had he remained a poor kid? Should stars be made more accountable than others because of their impact on society?

ENTERTAINMENT

From comic in Chicago's *Second City* theater group in 1971, through several years on television's hit show *Saturday Night Live*, to starring roles in the amazingly successful films *Animal House* and *The Blues Brothers* in the 1980s, John Belushi used one motto to guide his rise to the top of the entertainment world: "Fight, scream, refuse to do things." Cast in many roles during his short life, Belushi sometimes seemed unable to separate the parts he played from the life he led.

A long-time heavy drug user, Belushi insisted that he was "addicted to life." But those who knew how he craved drugs believed that he was much more "addicted to death." His untimely demise in 1982, from an overdose of a mixture of cocaine and heroin, seemed to show a greater desire to die than to live.

Belushi sincerely believed that his roles on television and in the movies as well as his own life style had meaning for all Americans. "My characters say it's okay to screw up," he told an interviewer. "People don't have to be perfect. They don't have to be real smart. They don't have to follow the rules. They can have fun. Most movies today make people feel inadequate. I don't do that."[2]

On stage and in real life, Belushi's behavior appeared to argue in favor of drugs. His message was clear: Drugs are good. You can do your own thing and still succeed. Nevertheless, his ruined marriage, the fifty thousand dollars a month he spent on drugs, the many enemies he made as he climbed the ladder to stardom, and his death at age thirty-three seemed to point out a different message: Relentless drug abuse has disastrous consequences.

After their deaths, some stars receive even more adulation than before. Their reputations become enhanced. Pop entertainers, such as Jimi Hendrix and Janis Joplin, were praised excessively after their early deaths from drug abuse. For them, lethal drug-taking became a kind of badge of distinction. People seemed to forget that drugs did not create their abilities or special qualities. Great artists and personalities had their talent developed long before they began drug use.

Drug expert Bob Meehan says that the Hollywood film industry has been strongly influenced by the drug culture. Some movies, he points out, advocate substance abuse. By their actions, the stars convey the impression that drugs are "exciting, rebellious, romantic, and hip," writes Meehan. He also notes that while films depict the pleasures of drugs, they deny the real problems that come with drug use.

According to Meehan, "Cheech and Chong films

explicitly advocate drugs." *Up in Smoke*, for example, is about lower-class youngsters who smoke dope and keep getting into trouble. Young audiences find the characters very attractive. They don't see any of the bad consequences of drug abuse; they are just aware of the "up" side. "Cheech and Chong," says Meehan, "are telling young people that taking drugs is good for them."[3]

In his book, *Beyond the Yellow Brick Road*, Meehan mentions other movies, including comedies, horror films, and romances, that show actors lighting up joints of marijuana or snorting cocaine. Meehan believes that young people who see these images can easily get the idea that drugs are fun. Nothing is shown about careers ruined, jobs lost, families torn apart, or children abandoned by "spaced-out" parents. The underlying message is that drug abuse is acceptable behavior; highly successful people do drugs and are none the worse for it.

The same message is demonstrated on television. George Gerbner, dean of the Annenberg School of Communications at the University of Pennsylvania, studies how the television medium helps set public taste. Television is so persuasive, he says, that most people think what they see on television is normal.

BUSINESS

In 1973, at age forty-seven, John DeLorean was a top executive at General Motors. He was earning over a half million dollars a year and had a good chance of becoming the number-one man at the giant corporation. At that point, however, the top businessman abruptly left General Motors and within one year announced the formation of DeLorean Motor Cars, Ltd., a new company to manufacture luxury automobiles.

Before long, DeLorean had a brand-new factory—

built for him in Northern Ireland by the British government—that was turning out twenty thousand cars a year. But he was only able to sell three thousand cars annually!

It took only a short time before DeLorean Motor Cars Ltd. owed $6 million to some three hundred creditors. Now desperate, DeLorean planned a fantastic way of making money. He contacted someone whom he believed to be active in the drug trade—but who was really an informant for the DEA. The deal they concocted was for DeLorean to put up about two million in cash to import into the United States huge quantities of heroin from Thailand and cocaine from South America. His contact would then take care of the sales and turn over the expected profit of $40 million to DeLorean, who would then use the money to rescue his failing company.

Unfortunately for DeLorean, when he flew to Los Angeles to complete the deal the police had enough evidence to arrest him on the spot. However, DeLorean was not convicted; some jurors from his trial felt the government had entrapped him into participating in the drug conspiracy, while other jurors said that the government had not proved its drug trafficking case against DeLorean.[4]

After the DeLorean case made the papers, Herbert London, of New York University, asked a class of high school students whether they would "sell illegal drugs in order to save a failing business enterprise." One student answered, "If I was in the same situation, I would definitely do it. I'd like to say that I wouldn't, but that would be lying, knowing true human nature." Another class member announced, "If they offered me a certain amount of money, then I would."

What do Americans learn from business deals based on drugs that make big bucks? Do they come to admire anything—including drug dealing—that makes money in our society? Or, do they realize that such deals are corrupt and damaging?

THE GETTING STRAIGHT MOVEMENT

Celebrities who have been involved with drugs sometimes want to use their experiences to prevent others from making the same mistake. Books, lectures, television appearances, and interviews are their way of capturing the public's attention. Perhaps their struggles with drug addiction will make it easier for others to find their way back to good health. The flood of materials has two main ideas—you can say no to drugs, and doing drugs is a harmful habit that can be broken.

In 1978, former first lady Betty Ford admitted a dependency on alcohol and painkillers. She shared the course of her hospital treatment with the public. The notoriety provided accurate information about drugs and their reactions, balanced with an understanding of why people use drugs. Dr. David Smith, an outstanding drug therapist, said: "Betty Ford has done more to get people in treatment than any government program." Larry Meredith, program chief of San Francisco's Community Substance Abuse Services, adds: "Betty Ford made it okay and respectable—almost in vogue—to have a problem and deal with it. She has been a national treasure."[5]

Great value comes from celebrities merely announcing that they solved their drug problems. Elizabeth Taylor and Johnny Cash openly admitted that they had been successfully treated for drug abuse. Richard Pryor spoke out frankly about how drugs had almost killed him. Ballet star Gelsey Kirkland wrote of her cocaine addiction and how she kicked it after leaving the American Ballet Theater in 1984. And actress Carrie Fisher, the star of such films as *Shampoo*, *Star Wars*, and *The*

Empire Strikes Back, explained both how she got hooked (wanting to be accepted by people who did drugs) and what made her stop (John Belushi telling her that she was like him).

Community drug-abuse prevention can take the form of organized programs like Nancy Reagan's "Just Say No" campaign or individual efforts. Always the object is the same—to provide good examples of mature behavior. But it also has other advantages. It helps change public attitudes that equate drug abuse with sophistication and it stops people from being unnecessarily harsh on drug users.

12

ETHICAL ISSUES

Frank is well known to the police in the small city in which he lives. Now twenty-four years old, he has been in trouble with the law for many years. The first charge—loitering for the purpose of using drugs—dates back to when he was only fifteen.

Since then the police have picked him up nearly a dozen times for drug-related crimes. Most of the time he either pays a small fine and is released or serves a short sentence of six months to a year in jail.

Early in 1988, a new police chief was appointed. One of his first actions was to start a campaign called "Project Clean Sweep." Its goal was to drive all drug dealers out of town. The police on the beat were ordered to track down all dealers and bring them in.

Just two days after Operation Clean Sweep was launched, Frank was walking along a downtown street. He didn't have any drugs on him. Yet suddenly a patrol car screeched to a stop next to him. "Freeze!" one cop ordered as he moved toward Frank, grabbing him roughly and clapping on a pair of handcuffs.

"Wha'cha doin' man?" Frank asked. "I'm clean. I didn't do nothin'."

"We'll see," growled the officer. While rifling through Frank's pockets with his right hand, the cop reached into his own pocket with his other hand. He pulled out a tightly wrapped package, somewhat bigger than a pack of cigarettes. Passing the package around, the policeman pretended to be pulling it from Frank's jacket pocket. Then he held it up in front of Frank's face. "I thought you said you were clean," the officer said with great sarcasm. "What's this?"

Frank's eyes widened. "I never saw that before," he protested. "That ain't mine. Hey, man, what is this, some sort of frame-up?"

The policeman winked at his partner. Then, turning back to Frank, he said, "Come on, Frank, you know we don't pull stuff like that. We just caught you red-handed. I'll bet you get twenty years on this one." And they hurried him into the patrol car and to the station house.

Despite his protests at the trial, Frank was found guilty on the faked evidence. He was sentenced to fifteen to twenty years at the state penitentiary. And the two officers who made the arrest were commended for nabbing a big drug offender.

Although Frank's story is not real, it illustrates how the authorities are sometimes under pressure to violate ethical standards and break the law to wage war against drugs. It also raises a very fundamental question: Is violating people's rights justifiable when protecting the community against drugs? Or is it better to stick to the letter of the law and risk letting drug criminals get away?

The American people are fed up with the problems caused by widespread drug abuse. A September 1985 poll showed that the public considers drug abuse the

An anti-crack rally takes place in Brooklyn, New York.

nation's number one problem. So government officials on all levels—local, state, and national—have been taking some strong measures to combat drugs. Although there have been some victories, by and large the war is being lost. This has led to even tougher strategies that have been sharply criticized. Chief among them are drug testing and increasing the penalties for drug violators.

DRUG TESTING

Late in the spring of 1986 all the firefighters and police officers in the city of Plainfield, New Jersey, were ordered to submit urine samples in a series of surprise drug tests. The urine samples were sent to a lab where they were examined for traces of illegal drugs. Sixteen firefighters and one police officer tested positive and were immediately discharged.

The fired workers went to court to challenge the ruling. The basis of their case was that drug testing by the Plainfield fire and police departments was not "reasonable" in terms of the Fourth Amendment to the United States Constitution.

The Fourth Amendment to the Constitution states:

> *The right of the people to be secure in their persons, houses, papers and effects, against unreasonable searches and seizures, shall not be violated, and no warrants shall issue, but upon probable cause, supported by oath or affirmation, and particularly describing the place to be searched, and the persons or things to be seized.*

On September 18, 1986, Judge H. Lee Sarokin of Federal District Court in Newark ruled that mandatory testing of government employees was unconstitutional.

In handing down his decision, Judge Sarokin commented, "In order to win the war against drugs, we must not sacrifice the life of the Constitution in the battle."[1]

At the 1985 Super Bowl, the New England Patriots unexpectedly lost to the Chicago Bears, 46 to 10. Rumor had it that the Patriots lost because their players were on drugs. As it turned out, drugs were not the problem, but Patriots' coach, Raymond Berry, asked the players to vote on voluntary drug testing. The measure passed by an overwhelming majority. The team members later withdrew their approval, though, when the Patriots' office released the names of six "admitted drug users."

In pointing out the danger of testing players and revealing the names of those who tested positive, lawyer Gerry Spence said, "A player is not required by law to give information. If he does under a guarantee of privacy, he enters a contract. If he is named, he could be a victim of breach of contract as well as a breach of privacy." In reply to those who don't agree, Mr. Spence said, "They forget that a football player's rights are also our rights. Where do they draw the line?"

In August 1985, the school board in Becton, New Jersey, suggested that drug testing be made part of the medical exam required of all high school students. Any students who tested positive would be placed in treatment.

According to the American Civil Liberties Union, the Becton school board was really saying, "Prove that you don't use drugs." In their opinion, this goes against the American system of justice, which holds that everyone is innocent until proven guilty. It deprives students of due process, the constitutional guarantee of a fair and impartial hearing, before being condemned. Even more, it teaches young people to "discount important principles of our government as mere platitudes." Eventually, on December 9, 1985, the New Jersey State Superior Court ruled in favor of the students.

There are some who believe that it is right and ethical to stamp out drug abuse with wholesale drug testing. Arthur Brill, spokesman for the President's Commission on Organized Crime, states that position: "There are no civil rights when it comes to taking drugs, none whatsoever."

Others hold that drug testing is not an ethical approach to solving the drug-abuse problem. Representative Peter Rodino (Democrat, New Jersey), Chairman of the House Judiciary Committee, presents that point of view in his statement: "Wholesale testing is unwarranted and raises serious civil liberties concerns."[2]

STRONG LEGAL MEASURES

During 1986, the New York City police began seizing the automobiles of suspected cocaine buyers and sending police teams into "head shops" to confiscate large numbers of the glass pipes commonly used for smoking crack. New York City Mayor Edward Koch wrote in the New York Law Journal that the actions were "legitimate applications of the law against an extremely serious threat." He said, "We should all exalt civil liberties. But we should also exact the right of society to protect its children and to defend itself."

Two weeks later, Norman Siegel and Richard Emery published a response in the same journal. They wrote, "Our purpose is to preserve individual liberty. Whenever a government program, no matter how well intentioned diminishes the rights of the individual, we scrutinize it carefully to determine whether a sufficiently compelling societal need justifies the attendant loss of individual rights."

According to Siegel and Emery, taking people's cars and making it hard to get glass pipes will not curb drug abuse. They oppose any approach that tells the public that "diluting constitutional rights is a panacea. Such an approach is a misguided cruel hoax which tears at the fabric of our free society."[3]

Increasing the number of drug arrests is commonly suggested as a way of solving the drug problem. In fact, the criminal-justice systems in many big cities, including the police, courts, and prisons, are completely overwhelmed by the volume of drug-related crimes and criminals they must handle.

Even adding more cops, district attorneys, judges, and prisons will not have very much of an impact. Many experts believe it will do little more than inconvenience the drug dealers. The reason is that the number of drug offenses and offenders is so high that it is virtually impossible to catch them all, give them fair trials, and have the guilty ones serve appropriate prison terms.

The nation relies on a system of so-called "revolving door" justice. The police bring in the drug dealers. They speed through the courts by plea bargaining, in which the defendant pleads guilty to a lesser charge and is given a lighter sentence without going through a lengthy jury trial. Then, since all the country's prisons are dreadfully overcrowded, the dealers are released, usually after serving no more than two-thirds of the sentence, and are back out on the streets.

New antidrug laws are presently sending waves of offenders into already overcrowded federal prisons. According to Stephen S. Trott, the Associate Attorney General, more than 28,000 spaces are needed to cope with the rising number of prisoners. Officials are concerned that without more space, their ability to arrest more drug traffickers will be jeopardized.

Some experts on criminal justice criticize the new

rash of arrests. They call it a "knee-jerk reaction" to public pressure for tough laws and stronger measures against crime. They question both its effectiveness and cost.

On the other hand, certain state governors and other lawmakers are urging Congress to create a death penalty for drug dealers. The idea shows how great the political pressure is to act on the drug menace.

Representative Gekas of Pennsylvania proposed an amendment to a House drug bill in late 1986 calling for the death penalty for murderers in drug-related killings who already have committed three Federal drug violations. Its purpose would be to send a powerful message to drug traffickers that the nation is serious in its determination to control the drug epidemic.

The editors of the *New York Times*, though, believe that so extreme a measure "is unworthy of civilized society. At the price of principle, the Gekas amendment mainly allows legislators to look tough."[4]

Opponents to more severe punishment also argue that longer sentences won't have more than a slight effect. The chance of arrest remains small, and only a third of those arrested on serious charges wind up in jail. The rest have charges dismissed or plead guilty to less serious crimes.

A NEW APPROACH

While most government officials keep working to win the drug war, some experts say that the situation is not warlike. They point out that overall, with the exception of cocaine, the consumption of drugs is declining. They attribute the true cause of increasing crime to family and neighborhood disintegration, not drug abuse. Violence and crime is a response to rootlessness and disorientation.

Others call for an end to talk about winning drug wars. "Start thinking about drugpeace instead of drugwar," writes Arnold Trebach of the School of Justice, American University, Washington, D.C. He is seeking "moderation, calm, and tolerance in dealing with drug abusers." Trebach goes on to say that "while the nation has serious problems of drug abuse, neither this generation of our adults or our children is in danger of being destroyed by chemicals."[5]

While some think it's time to take a new approach, most Americans believe we must continue to wage war against drugs. The reason is simple. People fear that widespread drug use is sapping our country's strength and vitality. They worry about the many connections between drugs and crime, poor health, loss of productivity and creativity, and a general decline in mental sharpness. They fear that abandoning the struggle against drugs is tantamount to committing national suicide.

Because it is important to protect society from drug addicts, dealers, traffickers, and suppliers, the war on drugs will probably continue. But because it is equally important to protect citizens—children and adults— from the "ravages" of the war, more effective ways will need to be found to prevent drug abuse and help users live productive and noncriminal lives.

NOTES

CHAPTER 1

1. John S. Lang and Ronald H. Taylor, "America on Drugs," *U.S. News and World Report*, 28 July 1986, p. 48–53.
2. Richard Halloran, "Student Use of Cocaine Is Up As Use of Most Other Drugs Drops," *The New York Times*, 8 July 1986, p. 26.
3. James Barron, "Use of Cocaine But Not Other Drugs Seen Rising," *The New York Times*, 29 September 1986, p. B6.
4. Peter Kerr, "Rich vs. Poor Drug Patterns Are Diverging," *The New York Times*, 30 August 1987, p. 1, 28.
5. Ibid.
6. Joseph A. Califano Jr., "A National Attack on Addiction Is Long Overdue," *The New York Times*, 15 March 1987, p. 28.
7. Ibid.
8. National Institute on Drug Abuse (NIDA). *Drug Abuse in the Workplace*. (Washington, DC: NIDA, 1986), p. 40–45.
9. Evan Thomas, "The Enemy Within," *Time*, 15 September 1986, p. 59–68.
10. Ibid.

11. Lang, p. 48–53.
12. Califano, p. 28.
13. Thomas, p. 59–68.

CHAPTER 2

1. James A. Inciardi, *The War on Drugs* (Palo Alto, CA: Mayfield, 1986), p. 12.
2. Inciardi, p. 16.
3. Inciardi, p. 18.
4. Inciardi, p. 20.
5. Jacob V. Lamar, "Crack," *Time*, 2 June, 1986, p. 16–18.
6. Peter Kerr, "High-School Marijuana Use Still Declining, U.S. Survey Shows," *The New York Times*, 24 February 1987, p. A21.
7. Richard Halloran, "Student Use of Cocaine Is Up as Use of Most Other Drugs Drops," *The New York Times*, 8 July 1986, p. 20.

CHAPTER 3

1. Richard Hughes and Robert Brewin. *The Tranquilizing of America* (New York: Harcourt, 1979).
2. James Barron, "Use of Cocaine," p. B6.
3. Ibid.
4. Peter Kerr, "High–School Marijuana Use Still Declining," p. A21.

CHAPTER 4

1. Rosalie Greenberg, M.D., "Child and Adolescent Marijuana Abuse," *Psychiatry Letter* 11 (June 1984): p. 1.

2. "Can Cocaine Conquer America: A Compilation," *Reader's Digest*, January 1987, p. 32–38.
3. Sidney Cohen, *The Substance Abuse Problem* (New York: The Haworth Press, 1981), p. 350.
4. "AIDS: The Surgeon General's Report of Acquired Immune Deficiency Syndrome," *Newsday* (special supplement), 3 February 1987.
5. Cohen, p. 153.
6. Evan Thomas, "The Enemy Within," p. 58–68.
7. John Chiles, *Teenage Depression and Suicide* (New York: Chelsea House, 1986), p. 22.
8. Chiles, p. 31.

CHAPTER 5

1. Stephen C. Joseph, M.D. (letter to the editor), "Intravenous-Drug Abuse Is The Front Line in the War on AIDS," *The New York Times*, 4 December 1986, p. 31.
2. "AIDS Infants Malformed," *The New York Times*, 12 August 1986, III p. 5.
3. Jane Gross, "The Most Tragic Victims of AIDS," *The New York Times*, 17 July 1987, p. 16.
4. Erica E. Goode and Joanne Silberner, "AIDS: Attacking the Brain," *U.S. News and World Report*, 7 September 1987, p. 48–49.
5. "Insurers' Study Sees AIDS Cost of $50 Billion," *The New York Times*, 5 August 1987, p. B24.
6. Peter Kerr, "Rich Vs. Poor," p. 1, 28.

CHAPTER 6

1. Evan Thomas, "The Enemy Within," p. 59–68.
2. Ibid.
3. James A. Inciardi, *The War on Drugs*, p. 116.

4. Department of Health and Human Resources. "Drug Abuse and Drug Abuse Research" (Washington, D.C.: Department of Health and Human Resources, 1984).
5. Inciardi, p. 169–170.
6. Inciardi, p. 126.
7. Inciardi, p. 129.
8. Peter Kerr, "New Violence Seen in Users of Cocaine," *The New York Times*, 7 March 1987, p. 29.
9. Peter Kerr, "Rich Vs. Poor," p. 1, 28.
10. Jacob V. Lamar, "Crack," p. 16–18.
11. Ibid.
12. Inciardi, p. 134.
13. Ibid.
14. Inciardi, p. 156.
15. National Institute on Drug Abuse (NIDA). *Drug Abuse in the Workplace*, 1986, p. 1–5.
16. Rosenbaum, Marsha. *Women on Heroin* (New Brunswick, NJ: Rutgers University Press, 1981).
17. Roger Thompson, "AIDS: Spreading Mystery Disease," *Editorial Research Report*, 9 August 1985.

CHAPTER 7

1. John S. Lang and Ronald H. Taylor, "America on Drugs," p. 48–53.
2. Department of the Treasury. "Drugs, Money Launderers and Banks" (Washington, D.C.: Department of the Treasury, 1986).
3. Michael Jackson and Bruce Jackson, *Doing Drugs* (New York: St. Martin's, 1983), p. 204.
4. Jackson, p. 204.
5. Jackson, p. 215.
6. Jackson, p. 205.
7. Ibid.
8. Department of the Treasury.
9. Department of the Treasury.

CHAPTER 8

1. James A. Inciardi, *The War on Drugs*, p. 184–185.
2. Jon Norheimer, "Officer Arrests Plaguing Florida," *The New York Times*, 3 August 1986, p. 23.
3. Allman, T. D., *Miami: City of the Future*. (New York: Atlantic Monthly Press, 1987), p. 83.
4. Inciardi, p. 191.
5. Ibid.
6. Ibid.
7. Jim Mulvaney, "Bolivians Fear Drug War, Not Drugs," *Newsday*, 31 July 1986, p. 13.

CHAPTER 9

1. Ellis, Barbara Gray, ed., *Drug Abuse from the Family Perspective* (Washington, DC: National Institute on Drug Abuse, 1980).
2. Richard H. Blum and Associates. *Society and Drugs* (San Francisco: Jossey-Bass, 1969).
3. National Institute on Drug Abuse (NIDA). *Drug Abuse Among American High School Students*. (Washington, D.C.: NIDA, 1985).
4. Michael Jackson and Bruce Jackson, *Doing Drugs*, p. 78.
5. National Institute on Drug Abuse (NIDA). *Addicted Women: Family Dynamics, Self Perceptions, and Support Systems* (Washington, D.C.: NIDA, 1979).
6. Kaplan, John. *The Hardest Drug* (Chicago: University of Chicago Press, 1983).
7. Peter Kerr, "Crack Addiction: The Tragic Toll on Women and Their Children," *The New York Times*, 9 February 1987, p. B1, 2.
8. Ibid.
9. Peter Kerr, "Babies of Crack Users Fill Hospital Nurseries," *The New York Times*, 25 August 1986 II, p. 1.

CHAPTER 10

1. Gilda Berger, *Drug Testing* (New York: Franklin Watts, 1987), p. 94.
2. Berger, p. 96.
3. National Institute on Drug Abuse (NIDA). *Drug Abuse in the Workplace*, 1986, p. 1–5.
4. Reginald Stuart, "Amtrak Crash Spurs Call for Random Drug Tests," *The New York Times*, 22 January 1987, p. A22.
5. Janice Castro, "Drugs on the Job: Battling the Enemy Within," *Time*, 17 March 1986, p. 52–61.
6. National Institute on Drug Abuse (NIDA), p. 1–5.
7. Berger, p. 86.
8. Castro, p. 52–61.
9. Abbot Laboratories. *Drug Abuse: It Affects Us All.* (New Brunswick, NJ: Abbot Laboratories, 1987).

CHAPTER 11

1. Frank Litsky, "Giants Taylor, in New Book, Says He Used Cocaine Often," *The New York Times*, 24 July 1987, p. A1, B16.
2. Evan Thomas, "The Enemy Within," p. 59–68.
3. Bob Meehan, *Beyond the Yellow Brick Road* (New York: Contemporary Books, 1984), p. 56.
4. *Facts on File*. (New York: Facts on File, 1984), p. 602.
5. "Getting Straight: How Americans Are Breaking the Grip of Drugs and Alcohol," *Newsweek*, 4 June 1984, p. 62–69.

CHAPTER 12

1. "The Battle Over Drug Testing," *The New York Times*, 19 October, 1986, p. 31.

2. Gilda Berger, *Drug Testing*, p. 49.
3. "ACLU Denounces Drug Testing Recommendations," *The New York Times*, 4 March 1986.
4. Robert G. Newman, M.D., "Pro and Con Drug Testing in the Workplace," *The New York Times*, 7 September 1986, p. 18.
5. Arnold S. Trebach, *The Great Drug War* (New York: Macmillan, 1987), p. 383.

SOURCES

NEWSPAPERS AND MAGAZINES

Los Angeles Times
"Cocaine Addiction Turns Out to Be an Equal-Opportunity Disease," 30 June 1987

Nation
"Crack," 1 June 1986

The New York Times
"Use of Cocaine, but Not Other Drugs Seen Rising," 29 September 1986
"Study Says Abuse of Cocaine May Cause Seizures," 29 September 1986
"Student Use of Cocaine is Up as Use of Most Other Drugs Drops," 8 July 1986
"High School Marijuana Use Still Declining. U.S. Survey Shows," 24 February 1987
"A National Attack on Addiction Is Long Overdue," 15 March 1987
"On the Drug Patrol: Hands Tell It All." 31 August 1987
"Rich Vs. Poor: Drug Patterns Are Diverging," 30 August 1987

"Cocaine's Vicious Spiral: Highs, Lows, Desperation," 17 August 1986

"A New, Purified Form of Cocaine Causes Alarm as Abuse Increases," 29 November 1985

"From Subway to Church Door, Panhandlers Are There," 31 July 1987

"Intravenous Drug Abuse Is the Front Line in the War on AIDS," 4 December 1986

"Bleak Lives: Women Carrying AIDS," 27 August 1987

"Insurers' Study Sees AIDS Cost of $50 Billion," 5 August 1987

"AIDS Infants Malformed," 12 August 1986

"New York's AIDS Program Shifts Focus to Drug Abusers," 23 October 1987

"AIDS Deaths in New York Are Showing New Pattern," 22 October 1987

"AIDS Spread Seen in Same Patterns," 11 October 1987

"Trying to Avoid an Insurance Debacle," 22 February 1987

"AIDS Virus: Experts Debate The Outlook for Those Infected," 8 September 1987

"A Crack Plague in Queens Brings Violence and Fear," 19 October 1987

"Crime at Kennedy: Scams, Drugs and the Mob," 21 October 1987

"Violent Crime Drops in '86 but Decline Is Slowing," 6 October 1987

"Trial of Suspected Cocaine Tycoon Set for Today," 5 October 1987

"Charges About Drugs and Other Crimes by the Police Shake Rockland Town," 7 August 1987

"West Virginia Mayor Is Indicted on Drug Charges," 1 August 1987

"Drugs Trace a Mayor's Rise and Fall," 24 August 1987

"Bolivians Fear Drug War, Not Drugs," 31 July 1986

"Chinese Now Dominate New York Heroin Trade," 9 August 1987

"Cocaine Billionaires," 8 March 1987

"Chasing the Heroin from Plush Hotel to Mean Streets," 11 August 1987

"Which War on Drugs?" 31 August 1987

"Cop Arrests Plaguing Florida," 3 August 1986

"Murder Verdicts in Drug Ring Case," 14 May 1987

"210 Fugitives Caught in National Drug Sweep," 14 May 1987

"17 Found Guilty in 'Pizza' Trial of a Drug Ring," 2 March 1987

"Code Signaled Police Thefts," 2 May 1987

"Drug Couriers Easy Targets," 8 May 1987

"New York's Biggest Crack Ring is Broken, U.S. Officials Say," 31 July 1987

"Fighting Narcotics Is Everyone's Issue Now," 10 August 1986

"War on Drugs Puts Strain on Prisons U.S. Officials Say," 25 September 1987

"Carrie Fisher, Novelist, Looks Back at the Edge," 14 August 1987

"Giants' Taylor, in New Book Says He Used Cocaine Often," 24 July 1987

"Rockets Discuss Drug Temptation," 15 January 1986

"On Drug Alert at an MX Missile Base," 28 January 1987

"Marijuana Doesn't Mix With Rail Safety," 17 January 1987

"Amtrak Crash Spurs Call for Random Drug Tests," 22 January 1987

"Study Urges New Measures to Combat Drugs," 8 March 1987

"New Violence Seen in Users of Cocaine," 7 March 1987

"Crack Addiction: The Tragic Toll on Women and Their Children," 9 February 1987

"Babies of Crack Users Fill Hospital Nurseries," 25 August 1986

"High AIDS Rate Spurring Efforts for Minorities," 2
August 1987
"Children With AIDS," 17 July 1987
"Crack Burdening a Justice System," 24 November 1986
"Growth in Heroin Use Ending as City Users Turn to
Crack," 12 September 1986
"Drug Influx a Strain on the Beat," 26 August 1986
"From Colombia to Queens: Shadowy Route of Co-
caine," 25 July 1986
"Drugs and Parents' Fear Taint Washington Heights,"
10 August 1986
"How Drugs Destroyed an Officer," 8 August 1986
"Drug Abusers Try to Cut AIDS Risk," 17 April 1985
"Extensive Use of Drugs Before 8th Grade Found in
New York," 18 October 1984
"Women and Cocaine: A Growing Problem," 18 Feb-
ruary 1985
"The Big Business of Illegal Drugs," 11 December 1983

New Republic
Review of *Wired* (the John Belushi story), 6 August 1984

Newsday
"AIDS: The Surgeon General's Report of Acquired Im-
mune Deficiency Syndrome," 3 February 1987
"Crack's Innocent Victims: the Babies," 8 August 1986

Newsweek
"A Ballerina's Dance of Death," 28 July 1986
"Cocaine Babies: Hooked at Birth," 28 July 1986
"Crack and Crime," 16 June 1986
"From Cars to Cocaine," 1 November 1982
"Getting Straight," 4 June 1984
"The Hawk's Toughest Fight," 3 August 1987

Psychiatry Letter
"Child and Adolescent Marijuana Abuse," June 1984

Psychology Today
"Marijuana in the Air: Delayed Buzz Bomb," February 1986

Reader's Digest
"Can Cocaine Conquer America?" January 1987
"The Mobs' Stranglehold on New York," November 1986

Time
"Crack," 2 June 1986
"Drugs on the Job," 17 May 1986
"The Enemy Within," 15 September 1986
"Striking at the Source," 28 July 1986

U.S. News and World Report
"American on Drugs," 28 July 1986
"Cocaine Spreads Its Deadly Net," 22 March 1982
"Federal Vs. Drug Runners: Game Gets Trickier," 4 October 1982
"Flood of Drugs—A Losing Battle," 25 March 1985

PUBLICATIONS

Abbot Laboratories. *Drug Abuse: It Affects Us All.* New Brunswick, N.J.: Abbot Laboratories, 1987.

Department of Health and Human Services. *Consequences of Maternal Drug Abuse.* Washington, D.C., 1985.

Department of Health and Human Resources. *Drug Abuse and Drug Abuse Research.* Washington, D.C., 1984.

Department of Health and Human Services. *Marijuana Effects on the Endocrine and Reproductive Systems.* Washington, D.C., 1984.

Department of the Treasury. *Drugs, Money Launderers and Banks.* Washington, D.C., 1986.

National Institute on Drug Abuse. *Current Research on the Consequences of Maternal Drug Abuse*. Washington, D.C., 1985.

National Institute on Drug Abuse. *Drug Abuse in Selected Metropolitan Areas*. Washington, D.C., 1982.

National Institute on Drug Abuse. *Drug Abuse in the Workplace*. Washington, D.C., 1986.

National Institute on Drug Abuse. *Drug Abuse from the Family Perspective*. Washington, D.C., 1980.

National Institute on Drug Abuse. *Drug Abuse Among American High School Students*. Washington, D.C., 1985.

New York Academy of Sciences Newsletter, Summer 1987.

BOOKS

Allman, T. D. *Miami: City of the Future*. New York: Atlantic Monthly Press, 1987.

Altman, Dennis. *AIDS in the Mind of America*. New York: Doubleday, 1986.

Baron, Jason D. *Kids and Drugs*. New York: Perigee, 1984.

Berger, Gilda. *Addiction*. New York: Franklin Watts, 1982.

Berger, Gilda. *Crack*. New York: Franklin Watts, 1987.

Berger, Gilda. *Drug Testing*. New York: Franklin Watts, 1987.

Blum, Richard H. and Associates. *Society and Drugs*. San Francisco: Jossey-Bass, 1969.

Chiles, John. *Teenage Depression and Suicide*. New York: Chelsea House, 1986.

Cohen, Sidney. *The Substance Abuse Problems*. New York: Haworth, 1981.

Hawley, Richard A. *The Purpose of Pleasure*. Wellesley, MA: Independent School Press, 1983.

Hughes, Richard and Robert Brewin. *The Tranquilizing of America*. New York: Harcourt, 1979.

Inciardi, James A. *The War on Drugs*. Palo Alto, CA: Mayfield, 1986.

Jackson, Michael and Bruce Jackson. *Doing Drugs*. New York: St. Martin's Press, 1983.

Jacobs, George and Joseph Kerrins. *The AIDS File*. Woods Hole, MA: Crowlech, 1987.

Johnson, Bruce. *Taking Care of Business*. Lexington, MA: Lexington Books, 1985.

Jones, Helen C. and Paul W. Lovinger. *The Marijuana Question*. New York: Dodd, Mead & Co., 1985.

Kaplan, John. *The Hardest Drug*. Chicago: University of Chicago Press, 1983.

Kirkland, Gelsey and Gregory Lawrence. *Dancing on My Grave*. New York: Doubleday, 1986.

Long, Robert Emmet, ed. *AIDS*. New York: Wilson, 1987.

Long, Robert Emmet. *Drugs and American Society*. New York: Wilson, 1986.

Meehan, Bob. *Beyond the Yellow Brick Road*. New York: Contemporary Books, 1984.

Polson, Beth. *Not My Kid*. New York: Arbor House, 1984.

Rosenbaum, Marsha. *Women on Heroin*. New Brunswick, NJ: Rutgers University Press, 1981.

Seymour, Richard R. *Drugfree*. New York: Facts on File, 1987.

Stone, Nanette, Marlene Fromme, and Daniel Kagan. *Cocaine*. New York: Crown, 1984.

Trebach, Arnold. *The Great Drug War*. New York: Macmillan, 1987.

INDEX

/143/

3